A NEW OWNER'S
GUIDE TO
SHIH TZU

JG-104

The Publisher wishes to acknowledge the following owners of the dogs in this book: Lynne Bennett, Debbie Burke, Janet H. Danner, Jean Kennedy Jameson, Claryce Johnson, Chris Jones, David F. Jones, Terri Kurinski, Kathy Kwait, Peggy Lowe, Patricia Mushrush, Elleen Nicholas, Kate O'Brien, Gay Payne, Ginger Raber, JoAnn Regelman, Sandra Richardson, Dee Shepherd, Earl and Xena Takahashi, Pam Tasker, John and Prudence Timney, Christopher Vicari, Emanuel Comitini, Linda and Roy Ward, Jennifer Lynn Winship, P. Michael Shea-Zackin.

Photographers: Baines Photography, Isabelle Francais, Earl Graham, Bernard W. Kernan, Richard Lowall, Robert Pearcy, Robert Smith, Luis F. Sosa, Karen Taylor, Missy Yuhl.

The author acknowledges the contribution of Judy Iby for the following chapters: Sport of Purebred Dogs, Identification and Finding the Lost Dog, Traveling With Your Dog, and Health Care for Your Dog.

Title page: Shih Tzu photograph by Isabelle Francais.

T.F.H. Publications, Inc.
One TFH Plaza
Third and Union Avenues
Neptune City, NJ 07753

www.tfh.com

A New Owner's
Guide to
SHIH TZU

JoAnn Regelman

Contents

2002 Edition

A Shih Tzu wants nothing more than to be adored by its owner.

A Shih Tzu puppy is easy to fall in love with.

A Shih Tzu's coat will need daily grooming to keep it looking its best.

Nylabones® are safe chewing pacifiers

Owning two Shih Tzu is more fun than just one.

DEDICATION

To my husband, Joe,
without whose love and support
I could never have kept my castle of Shih Tzu
nor finished this little book on their behalf.
JoAnn

EDITOR'S NOTE

In October 1991, with the encouragement of a mutual friend, Boxer breeder Rick Tomita, I invited JoAnn Regelman, the Corresponding Secretary of the American Shih Tzu Club, to author a new book on the breed. JoAnn responded most enthusiastically, and we began corresponding.

JoAnn's "castle of Shih Tzu" took so much of her time that there was never time for writing. Fortunately, her husband Joe helped with the dogs so that JoAnn could make time to write this book, the first book she ever attempted. Never before had I encountered such a passionate fancier with so much love and dedication for her breed (which she truly believed were "fur people"). She loved nothing more than a Shih Tzu puppy—and she had many of them all the time!

When Joe died suddenly, the book stopped. We extended the deadline; we extended the extension.

Finally in late March 1995, the manuscript arrived accompanied by a note from JoAnn saying, "Here's my baby. Off to hospital for tests. Call me when you receive this."

This book is a lasting tribute to JoAnn's love and dedication to the Shih Tzu. It stands in memory of her husband Joe, as well as in memory of her. JoAnn died only a few months after submitting the manuscript. She is missed by this editor, her children, and the many "fur people" that once proudly paraded around her home.

Andrew De Prisco
Editor
March 1996

A Shih Tzu will capture the heart of everyone it comes in contact with.

INTRODUCTION to the Shih Tzu

Many centuries ago, it is believed that somewhere in the mountains of Tibet, a small, heavy-coated, playful, fascinating, adorable dog named Shih Tzu (pronounced Sheed-Zoo) was bred. When Shih Tzu is loosely translated it means "lion dog." As with all the Oriental breeds, it is very difficult to pinpoint their exact origin or their exact beginnings. They have been depicted as long ago as 600 AD in Oriental works of art and paintings. Legend traces the origin of the breed to the temples of Tibet where these little "lion dogs" were highly revered. It is known that during the Manchu Dynasty (17th century) a pair of Shih Tzu was presented to distinguished visitors as a token of goodwill and good luck.

During the Chinese revolution in 1911, the Shih Tzu became virtually extinct in mainland China. Fortunately for the Shih Tzu, the profit-seeking eunuchs of the Dowager Empress sold some of the palace's dogs to wealthy Chinese as well as foreigners. The death of the Empress in 1908

It is hard to believe that the beautiful little Shih Tzu became almost extinct. What would the dog world be without this wonderful little Lion Dog?

Three seven-month-old puppies bred by Earl and Xena Takahashi of Xeralane Shih Tzu.

ended an era for the Shih Tzu, though the breed was able to continue in the Scandinavian countries, Holland and England. Eventually they made their way to the United States, where they were recognized by the American Kennel Club in 1969.

THE UNIQUE AND COLORFUL SHIH TZU

Shih Tzu come in many colors and sizes. The AKC standard states that they are to weigh between 9 and 16 pounds and stand anywhere from 8 to 11 inches. Of course there are exceptions to every rule, and we do occasionally see dogs that vary from those dimensions.

As a breeder, I try to fit the right dog into the right home. If a family has two or three rambunctious children, they need a dog with a little size and bone to romp and play with the kids. A home with adults is great for the slightly smaller dogs. Trust your breeder to tell you which puppy is the leader of the pack, and which one is the more quiet one. Be they quiet or crazy, all Shih Tzu will love you forever and follow you to the ends of the

This is Can.Ch. Xeralane's Spellbinder bred and owned by Earl and Xena Takahashi.

earth. Shih Tzu are desperate to please you; they are not demanding but loving and loyal. If you do not have time to hold them, please just let them sit under your chair or at least near you. When I sit at the table, I cannot move my chair or put my feet down on the floor—I

It is only through dedication and responsible breeding that the Shih Tzu has become the spectacular and endearing breed that we know today.

am surrounded by my hairy friends. They all need to be close to mom.

The standard for Shih Tzu says all colors are acceptable. You seldom see an all white Shih Tzu, usually there is some color on the dog somewhere, but any colors or markings are allowed. My first two Shih Tzu were gold and white, the third was gold/brindle and white, and the fourth was black and white. The favorite colors seem to be gold and white and black and white, with a white blaze and beard, white feet, and a white tip on their tails. Classically they would be marked with a white shawl and a colored saddle. Needless to say, we have to take what God provides. There is no way to order a special color or perfect markings. Many Shih Tzu are solid gold with a black mask, some are all black. Whatever color or however marked, each and every one of them is special.

OWNING a Shih Tzu

Owning a Shih Tzu can be the most delightful experience any family can embark upon. Taking a Shih Tzu into your home is very much like adopting a child. I believe Shih Tzu are really not dogs, but wonderful little people in hair-suits. Once a Shih Tzu comes into your life, you will never want to live without one again. They crawl into your lap, wrap themselves around your heart, and you become totally theirs.

ARE YOU READY TO COMMIT TO A DOG?

Deciding to take a dog into your home should not be taken lightly. The life expectancy of a Shih Tzu is 14 to 16 years, which is a longtime commitment. You must also decide if you can take proper care of your new family friend. Aside from the initial purchase of the dog, you will have visits to the veterinarian for inoculations and spaying or neutering, food, toys, and, in the case of this breed, you will have grooming to deal with. Any coated breed, like the Shih

Shih Tzu require more care due to their long coat. If you are not prepared to groom this breed properly or have it done professionally, perhaps this is not the breed for you.

Shih Tzu are very accommodating dogs that prefer to take life easy. The best place for a Shih Tzu is on your bed, couch, or in your arms.

Tzu, must be groomed to keep the dog clean and in good health.

ACCOMMODATING THE SHIH TZU

One question I am asked many times is "Are Shih Tzu good apartment dogs?" In reality, I do not know of another breed that is as easy in a small environment. They can be easily paper trained for life, if you so wish. If I lived in the city on the 11th or 34th floor, I know I would not like to hop out of bed at the crack of dawn, get dressed, hit the elevator and head for the street while my poor dog stood there with its legs crossed. Shih Tzu do not like to go out in bad weather anyhow, so to not have to go out at all suits them fine. City streets can also be extremely dirty and disease ridden, and usually are not the most desirable place to be walking your little dog.

I do not want to say that Shih Tzu are innately lazy dogs, but the least amount of effort they must put into something, the better. After all, Shih Tzu are meant to be companions—they do not have to do anything else. The best place for a Shih Tzu is on your bed, on your lap, or on the couch.

Ch. Xeralane's Pursuit O'Happiness. Bred and owned by Earl and Xena Takahashi of Xeralane Shih Tzu.

Always supervise your child when playing with your Shih Tzu and be sure to teach the proper way to handle the dog.

As for exercise, they get plenty just following you around. As I have said before, they just want to be near you. The little amount of running around that they do is all that they need. They will always welcome a trip outside and a romp in the park, if you want to take them, but no five-mile hikes. You would be hiking home all alone with a Shih Tzu in your arms. They were also never meant to run a race. Your sweet, affectionate, face-kissing little lover will live wherever you ask it to, just make sure it is warm, loved, and healthy, with a good meal in its tummy and a cookie at bed time. Your life will never be the same again, and you will wonder what you did before the little hairball came into your life.

PREPARING for Your New Shih Tzu

Y ou will need to prepare so the puppy will be able to adjust to its new home easily. When you purchase the puppy, you should receive a list of equipment you need to have and then make a trip to the pet-supply store. You may want to crate train your puppy. The crate you choose should have a wire floor. This is so that if the puppy has an accident in the crate it does not have to sit in it. Crate training is a wonderful and very satisfactory way to housetrain a puppy. Puppies like their crates; they are like their own private houses. Dogs feel very secure in their crate; it equates to the den for wild dogs and is their own space. It is also a very safe place for your puppy to be when you are not home, or when there is too much going on in your home to keep an eye on what this busy little creature is up to. All puppies are very curious and can get themselves into trouble.

You will need to get puppy food. Find out what your puppy was eating and continue feeding the same food. Most breeders use good quality-food and are happy to recommend a specific brand that they feed. You will need a food dish for your puppy. I find Shih Tzu like low, flat dishes. This is because their noses are too short and they have a hard time breathing and eating at the same time from deep dishes. I advise owners to get a one-quart glass water bottle. All show Shih Tzu drink from water bottles. It keeps their faces clean

Shih Tzu puppies will try to get into whatever they can...including your gym bag!

and dry. Puppies can learn this all by themselves and seem to prefer it to a bowl. It also helps keep your floors dry, as when they drink from a bowl they get their little hairy faces all wet.

Your new Shih Tzu puppy should be fed the same food that it has been used to.

A steel comb and wire pin brush are also two very necessary requirements for a Shih Tzu puppy. You will also want to get a squeaky toy or two and a chew device. Make sure it is one with knuckles, not the skinny string ones which can get very slimy and slip down a puppy's throat and choke it. There are a great variety of Nylabone® products available that veterinarians recommend as safe and healthy for your dog or puppy to chew on. A puppy-gate can be very useful to keep your new pet in the kitchen. I find that puppies really resent a door shut in their face, but the gate does not make them feel so isolated from everyone when they are alone. You may also want to get a collar and a leash—the sooner you

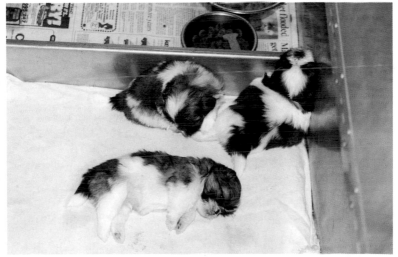

A full belly will put any Shih Tzu to sleep.

Although this litter of nursing Shih Tzu look adorable, breeding is highly specialized and should be left to professionals.

start lead training, the better. Puppies can get very stubborn about walking on a lead if you wait too long to train them.

Taking Your Puppy Home

Taking a new puppy home is very exciting. When you pick up your puppy, you should receive a health record and explanation of what shots have been given and what ones are still needed. It is most important to follow these instructions carefully. Without all his shots, your puppy could become ill and die. You may also be advised to spay or neuter your new pet. The best time to do this is at six months. It is not necessary for a female to come into season first. This belief is really an old wives' tale, and your bitch will never know what she has missed. The American Kennel Club is advising owners to spay or neuter their pets and so are most reputable breeders. By spaying your female you will avoid the possibility of her getting uterine cancer or mammary tumors. A male will avoid the possibility of testicular cancer and prostate trouble if he is neutered. You should also receive a contract with a guarantee on the puppy and a record of who the puppy's parents are, date of birth, and any other important information you may require.

This is "Bean" Ch. China's Extra Special in a casual pose.

At this time you should go over all the instructions on feeding, bathing, coat care, and housetraining, checking to see if you got all the puppy's needs and are ready to assume your responsibility with your new little hairball. I have printed out my instructions for everyone to take with them. I found that most people were so excited that they promptly forgot half of what I told them and were on the phone within a few hours. When you take a puppy into a new home it is very important to remember that it is all completely new and strange to this little creature. The pup will most likely spend a considerable amount of time exploring its new space. If it is time for a meal or treat, this is a good way to make the pup feel at home. Puppies also need a considerable amount of sleep. They will run and play and act adorable—and suddenly just crash on the floor and go to sleep. It is very important to let them nap, I always tell little children that puppies grow while they are sleeping, so they have to leave them alone to rest. They cannot play 24 hours a day.

Provide your puppy with plenty of safe toys to keep him from chewing your belongings.

If you are using a crate, show the puppy where his new house is. I suggest putting food and water and toys into the crate when the puppy is to be shut in. It will make him feel more at home when he has something to amuse himself with. The loneliness does not seem to be so awful then. A trick that works well at night when you have a sad, crying puppy is to put the crate into your bedroom or one of the kids' rooms. It seems to calm the puppy when he can at least see someone and know he has not been left completely alone. Imagine if you had just been taken away from all your sisters and brothers and your mom. How awful would you feel if you were stuck all alone in the kitchen in the dark? I would cry too.

Any puppy that has been asleep will need to be taken to its papers or outside immediately upon waking. Puppies always have to relieve themselves when they awaken. One important thing to remember is that it is not the puppy that is trained, it is the owner. All puppies will have an accident or two in their new home, you just have to forgive them. They soon learn what you want them to do, and where you want them to do it. It does not do any good to chastise them for accidents unless you catch them in the act. In that case you should tell the puppy "no," pick him up, and move him to the newspaper or to your chosen place outdoors.

Any of my puppies that are born after September do not go outside until spring. By the time they have had their first shot and are allowed to mix with the other dogs, it is much too cold to let them outside. They are paper trained. I do insist that people who

Rainy days and lots of naps go hand in hand for any Shih Tzu.

take my puppies in late fall or winter, keep their puppies on paper until spring. Dogs do not catch colds, but they do get pneumonia. Once they have reached six months, I feel the danger has passed, and they can go outside anytime. My dogs are crazy to get out in the snow, they come in

For the most privacy your Shih Tzu should be placed in its crate or in its own bed.

looking like little Abominable Snowmen and need to be defrosted, but they are sure to have fun rolling and plowing in the snow. Shih Tzu seem to have a real aversion to rain. On rainy days, I can barely get my "kids" out of their beds and comforters. They will take one look out the door and then one look at me as if to say, just spread out a little more newspaper mom. You will find that it does not take long for you and the puppy to settle into a routine, and your life will never be the same. Living with a Shih Tzu is like living with a clown. They can amuse you all day with their antics and love and kisses. I always tell people that are considering the possibility of two Shih Tzu at the same time to go for it, they will never need to go to the movies again—just sit back and watch the dogs.

PURCHASING a Shih Tzu

Before you venture out to look for a new puppy or puppies (Shih Tzu are great in pairs), you should follow a few rules. Buying a dog should not be done on the spur of the moment. There are very specific places you can call to receive advice on where to go and whom you should talk to.

1. Call the American Kennel Club for a referral, they will refer you to the national breed club. In England, The Kennel Club can provide a referral as well.
2. Call a local veterinarian, many times he will have a client who breeds Shih Tzu.
3. Inquire local all-breed dog clubs that may have referral services.
4. Talk to your friends and get a referral from them. If they have acquired a puppy and are happy, it should help you make a decision.

Most of these places will lead you to someone who has nice, sound, healthy puppies. You will find that most breeders do not have a constant supply of puppies, so you may have to get on a waiting list. Good things are worth waiting for.

THAT SPECIAL PUPPY

You have found a breeder who has a litter of puppies, and the day you have waited for is here. You arrive at the breeder's home, and usually will be greeted by a clan of small, tail-wagging, hairy rugs. Shih Tzu all want to be the first one to the door to greet everyone. It is the one time my dogs will really push each other out of the way to be first. After the kisses and oohs and aahs, you will be shown the babies. Depending on the age of the puppies, you may or may not be able to handle them at this time. Most breeders do not allow strangers to handle their pups before they have had their first shot, and you may have to content yourself with seeing the proud mom and letting the breeder show you the puppies at that time. Puppies must be protected before anyone other than their family can touch them. They are very vulnerable to disease, as the only immunity they have at

All Shih Tzu have irresistible personalities. You may find yourself coming home with two.

that time is from their mother. If they received their first shot at six or seven weeks, you should be able to play with them.

Once you have decided on that special puppy, unless it is old enough to be self-sufficient, it may have to stay with its littermates and mother (dam). I do not let my puppies go to their new homes until they are at least 12 weeks old. Shih Tzu are a toy breed, weighing only 4 to 6 ounces when they are born, and must be allowed to grow and mature before they can make a good transition to a new home and family. You should be able to go back and visit and play with your new baby and get to know it while you are impatiently waiting to take it home. I always invite people to come back so they can have the pleasure of watching their new family member change. Most people are amazed if they have seen a three- or four-week-old puppy, and then come back at seven

Your purebred Shih Tzu puppy will grow up to look very much like his parents.

Shih Tzu puppies are smooth coated when they are born, and it does not take long for that wonderful fuzz to grow.

weeks and see how much it has grown, and how much hair it has at this time. Shih Tzu puppies are smooth coated when they are born, and it does not take long for all that wonderful fuzz to grow. Each day it gets longer and longer. By the time they are three months old, they have grown what looks like a chrysanthemum on their little faces, and their bodies are abundant with the most wonderful silky coat.

GROOMING Your Shih Tzu

You and your puppy have settled into a routine and now it is time to start daily grooming. It is wise to spend some time each day with your Shih Tzu in the care of its coat. This can be a very rewarding experience for both of you, or it can become a horror. A Shih Tzu puppy must be taught to enjoy being groomed. It is very important not to give in to every little whimper or whine. You must be firm and make sure you gently let the puppy know you are boss, and soon the resistance will stop and you will both have a very nice time together. Even if you do not choose to groom the dog yourself, and take it to a groomer, it will become someone else's nightmare if the dog is not properly trained to be groomed. Ten minutes a day will give you and the puppy time to become accquainted with the comb and brush. I truly enjoy the time I spend alone on a one-to-one basis with each dog, giving my attention only to that dog, and it to me. It is also a time to get lots of extra kisses—Shih

Each Shih Tzu has a different texture of hair, growth rate and staining quotient, and some require different grooming methods than others.

Tzu are the best in the world at giving kisses. They are so trusting. It is important that you do not turn grooming into something unpleasant to them. Take time and have patience: you will be rewarded in the end with that beautiful little prince or princess.

An easy way to groom your puppy is to lay the dog on your lap on its side and gently start brushing (a pin brush with a padded cushion should be used) from the underside of the body. Brush in layers until you have reached the top

Shih Tzu are very trusting and it is therefore important that grooming always be a pleasant experience for them.

of the coat at the part. After the body coat is brushed, you will need to brush the legs, again starting at the bottom of the leg near the foot, and brushing the coat until you have

Your Shih Tzu's coat must be clean and dry before you ever begin to work with it. A dirty coat should never be brushed!

Face and beard hair grows more slowly than body hair in most cases. Be exceptionally careful when dealing with this area.

reached the top of the leg. Then you can use the comb (a steel comb with two sizes of pins is best) to comb through all the hair to make sure there are no mats or snarls left in the coat. If you do not brush and comb to the skin, you will end up with a truly unsightly matted mess of a dog. The mats can become very uncomfortable to the dog, and they can develop hot spots (sores) under them.

Each day you should clean any matter away from the eyes with a soft cloth. You can wash the face if it is soiled, and then comb through with a fine-tooth comb. About every three weeks, the nails should be clipped (a cat nail scissors or guillotine nail clipper may be used) and the pads trimmed (hair scissors or blunt-end scissors may be used if you are afraid to use sharp-end scissors). The nails should be clipped evenly with the bottom of the dog's pads.

This must be done very carefully. If you cut the nail too short (into the quick), the nail will bleed. If this should occur, a coagulant applied to the nail will stop the bleeding. The hair between the pads should be trimmed out, if not it will mat and cause the dog pain when walking.

THE BATH

A Shih Tzu can be bathed as often as once a week if you so desire, as long as a good conditioner is used to keep the skin from drying out. It is not detrimental to the dog or the coat to be bathed that often. They are very vain little dogs and like to be neat and clean. I feel that my dogs feel great after their bath and just love to be told how beautiful they are.

Before you bathe your Shih Tzu you should brush through the coat. If you wet any mats or snarls they will become set, as in concrete, and you will not be able to remove them without professional help, or the aid of the scissors. If you start cutting out mats, your dog will no longer look quite as neat as it should, rather like an unmade bed.

Put the dog in the sink and, using an attachment hose or your sink sprayer, gently wet the dog all over its body. Be very careful not to get water up the nose or in the ears—water up that little nose is very uncomfortable, and water in the ears can cause infection. Shih

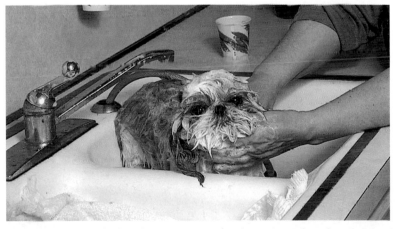

Shih Tzu can be bathed as often as once a week as long as a good conditioner is used to keep the skin from drying out.

29

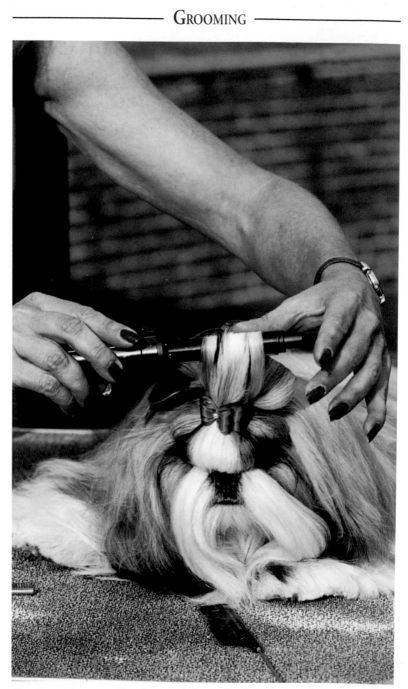

Groomers may use curling irons to help set the Shih Tzu's topknot.

Tzu have drop ears, and inside is a dark, moist, warm place perfect for infection. With the water turned off, apply a good-quality dog shampoo (for the face, you may feel more secure using one of the tearless shampoos available at your local pet store) and wash the dog. Shih Tzu have hair, not fur, and should be shampooed as you would shampoo your own hair. After the shampoo, rinse well. If you do not rinse the dog well it will have itchy skin. Apply a conditioner to the coat, work it in well and rinse again. Towel the dog with a Turkish towel and blow dry. Shih Tzu are not drip-dry dogs. If you

Shih Tzu have hair, not fur. Their coat should be shampooed as you shampoo your own hair.

do not have a table dryer, it may take two people, one to hold the dryer and one to brush and comb. While the dryer is blowing the hair, it is important to brush each layer of the body and leg coat. Usually behind the ears and the face are the last parts to dry: The face because Shih Tzu do not really enjoy the dryer in their face, and the coat behind and around the ears because it is very thick.

Once the dog is all dry and if it is still in coat (has its hair), you will need to carefully part the facial hair and pin up the topknot (part between eyes) with small elastic bands. Latex bands are preferred, as they do not break the hair. It is of the utmost importance to keep the topknot hair out of a Shih Tzu's eyes. Hair constantly rubbing on the eye can cause a great deal of damage to the eye. I advise my pet puppy owners to cut the topknot off at about four months of age unless they are truly dedicated to keeping the face combed and the topknot up.

This would be the time to pluck out any excess hair from the ears (a hemostat is used). Ear plucking is necessary on many Shih Tzu, as they tend to grow large amounts of hair down in their ear. You will see the hair protruding from the ear canal. If this hair is not removed on a regular basis, the wax will build up in the ear canal and cause smelly, sick ears. A little ear powder is placed into the ear, and the hair is extracted with the hemostat. If you do not feel comfortable, perhaps your veterinarian should be asked to pluck the ears. The dog's nails should be clipped, pads trimmed, and the hair around the anus trimmed. If this hair is not kept trimmed the dog can run into severe problems with fecal matter stuck to the hair, and the dog can become impacted.

PROFESSIONAL GROOMERS

Of course all this bathing and blowing and brushing can be totally avoided if you choose to use a professional groomer. By the age of four months it will be necessary to either pin up the topknot or cut it off. I do not advise that a puppy under the age of four months be taken to the groomer, you never know what other dogs have brought into the shop on any given day. Therefore you should know at least how to keep your young dog neat and clean. Usually by six months of age, they have grown sufficient hair to warrant

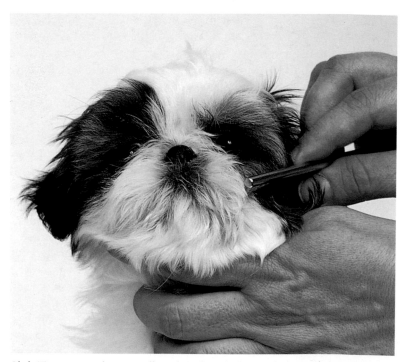

Shih Tzu puppies learn to allow their faces be brushed or combed early on.

Taking your Shih Tzu to a professional groomer will keep it looking its very finest.

having a puppy cut. This should be done by a competent groomer. A puppy cut needs to be redone about every six weeks to be kept in order.

SUMMARY
To sum up the grooming of a Shih Tzu:
1. Brushing daily or at least every other day.
2. Cleaning the face and eyes daily.
3. Weekly or bi-weekly baths.
4. A visit to the groomer to have topknot trimmed, ears plucked and nails done (or you may do ears and nails) at four months.
5. A puppy cut at six months to be re-cut every six weeks.

If you are truly dedicated to brushing hair (carefully and to the skin each day), by all means grow a beautiful long coat, but do not make your dog suffer through long battles with de-matting by you or a groomer because you have neglected to brush for a few days. No matter how good your groomer is, a Shih Tzu can get very matted in a matter of three or four days if in full coat. My honest recommendation from the heart is a puppy cut at six months. It makes you and your dog happier.

CARING for Your Shih Tzu

I t is obvious that a responsible dog owner needs to have a doctor for their new family member. Just as you need to take your child to the pediatrician, your dog needs check-ups, and you need someone to count on in an emergency. Finding the right veterinarian is not always easy. Your first choice might be the doctor that your breeder uses. After all, he has been taking care of the puppies and their relatives, probably for years, and would be aware of the puppy's health record. If a new puppy owner does not live in the same area as I do, I suggest that they check with their neighbors and friends who have pets. Pet lovers will be the first to tell you who treats them and their pets well.

You also want to be sure to find a veterinarian who understands and likes toy dogs. Believe it or not, they are not all lovers of small dogs. It is also important to have a veterinarian who is on call 24 hours a day, either through his own practice or through a competent referring doctor. You never know when you could have that emergency. On a sunny Sunday afternoon when you are out in the yard and the dog gets stung by a bee, it is very comforting to know you can get an answer on the phone to your question—What do I do now?

Every puppy should visit the veterinarian when a new owner takes possession. You should receive a health record and a health guarantee in the contract you receive with your puppy. When my puppies leave me at 12 weeks, they will have received two of their three baby shots. The very basic shots are for distemper, hepatitis, leptospirosis, parainfluenza, and parvovirus. A puppy will need a third shot at 16 weeks to complete its immunity. The next recommended visit should be at six months, at which time the puppy should receive its rabies shot and be spayed or neutered. At 16 months, or one year after the puppy shots are completed, the dog needs to return for a checkup, and a booster shot (DHLPP). This should continue for the rest of its life. The first rabies shot is only good for one year, thereafter rabies will be given every three years. Depending on where you reside, heartworm preventative may be given during the mosquito

This is Ch. Ultra's Guilty As Sin "Felon." Owned by Elleen Nicholus.

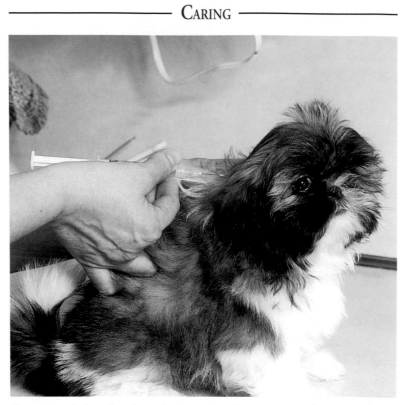

Be sure to ask the seller about the immunizations your puppy has received prior to your bringing him home.

season. Besides regular checkups, occasional cleaning of the dog's teeth should be done. In recent years, there has been a general problem with Lyme disease. There is now a vaccine for this disease, and also depending upon the area in which you live, a vaccination for Lyme disease should be given.

SPECIFIC HEALTH PROBLEMS OF THE BREED

On a whole Shih Tzu are a very tough little breed. They are the largest of the toy breeds, the males usually being a slightly larger-boned, heavier dog than the females. I do not spend a great deal of time visiting my veterinarian due to ill dogs. My visits are for C-sections, shots, or maintenance for my senior citizens. Older dogs do require more care than young dogs. Checking daily to make sure that the eyes are clear, there is no problem with an overgrown rear, or the dog is not lethargic is a good idea.

Due to the short muzzles on Shih Tzu, many puppies may have pinched nostrils (stenotic nares). This usually starts when the puppies begin to teethe at six to eight weeks of age and lasts until they are five or six months old. There may also be a clear, watery discharge from the nose at that time, which is of no concern. Pinched nostrils may also cause puppies to sniffle, snort, or snore. My first Shih Tzu was named "Snuff"—can you guess why? When he was a baby he made the cutest sounds, which were caused by his pinched nostrils. He did outgrow them, but he was "Snuff" for life. If at any time your puppy should have mucus, or thick, colored discharge from the nostrils, that would be cause to visit your veterinarian.

Many Shih Tzu puppies have umbilical hernias. They are hereditary in the breed, or are sometimes caused by birth trauma. Most umbilical hernias that are small in diameter do heal over or close up by themselves by the time the dog is six or

A daily overall check of your Shih Tzu will keep it in its best health. The coat of this breed is a special consideration and should be checked thoroughly.

Any change in your Shih Tzu's personality is cause notify your veterinarian immediately.

eight months old. An umbilical hernia is like an outie belly button, where the puppy was attached to its mother. It is nothing more than a small globule of fat that protrudes through an opening in the gut. In the case that the opening is as large as a dime or larger, it may require repair. Most veterinarians will wait to do the repair until the puppy is spayed or neutered. In the case of the female, the incision to spay needs to be slightly larger to accommodate the repair. In the case of the male puppy, the hernia surgery is done at the same time as neutering but with a different incision. The only time to become concerned about an umbilical hernia is if it should become red or sensitive to the touch, which means that it is causing your puppy some pain and could be strangulated (meaning that the hernia has become smaller and the fat globule has slipped through the hole and cannot get back in). This usually means surgery must be done at once.

I do not include the following information to frighten you, but to hopefully make you a better consumer and dog owner. Approximately 18 years ago, when I first heard about kidney disease (renal kidney failure) in my breed, I vowed to do my best to make sure that I would not produce any puppies that would get sick, suffer and die. I discussed kidney biopsies with my veterinarian, who really did not want to participate in the testing. He said that he "did not want to cut up my healthy dogs." After convincing him that it really meant a great deal to me, he contacted the research veterinarian at the University of Pennsylvania to discuss how the surgery was to be done. It is major abdominal surgery and not to be taken lightly. The first dog I biopsied was my beautiful little Best in Show champion "Pepper." He came through with flying colors, and we went on from there to biopsy most of my adult dogs hoping that if I bred from clear unaffected dogs, my future generations would also be healthy. I have since kept up to my testing, although we now can use ultrasound to check for immature kidneys and do not have to do surgery. I have been very fortunate not to have to watch my dogs become ill.

Shih Tzu, like all pets, rely on their owners for care. It is our responsibility as good owners to give them everything they need to live happy and healthy lives.

Eleven-month-old "Dusty" owned by Claryce Johnson and Bred by Roxi Kastner.

Most often would-be sires and dams are screened for hereditary disease to ensure a healthy litter.

As in several other breeds of dogs, renal dysplasia is a problem in Shih Tzu. It is a disease that causes the kidneys to develop improperly. It is hoped that you will seek out a breeder who has tested his breeding stock to screen out any dogs that are possibly affected. There has been a great deal of research done in the breed on kidney disease, but the answers seem to be elusive. A severely affected dog will not develop properly, will consume inordinate amounts of water (an effort to flush their kidneys), and the urine will be dilute (white or clear in color). They will usually be lethargic, at times throw up, and, in most cases, not be interested in food. There are tests a veterinarian can do to check on the kidney function. Bun, urine specific gravity, and creatine tests will help to disclose a dog that has very little kidney function left. There are many dogs that are mildly or moderately afected with kidney disease and, if not bred or stressed (as with a show career or being used for breeding), can possibly live normal lives. It is only the severely affected dogs that do not live.

Immune-related diseases sometimes affect Shih Tzu. If the thyroid functions are not normal, you may see itchy skin, waxy ears, oily skin and coat, clammy skin, sweaty armpits, smelly ears, obesity, hyperpigmentation (black or dark patches on the skin), and laziness. There is a very simple blood test that will give you the exact thyroid function or malfunction of your dog.

This condition can be controlled by giving your dog daily thyroid medication as in humans.

Another immune related disease is von Willebrand's disease. This causes the blood to clot improperly. This can also be tested for with a blood test. Any dog that requires surgery should be pre-tested for this problem. Many bitches have lost their lives after whelping a litter of puppies. Their immune system does not function properly, and they hemorrhage internally and die. It is another good reason to spay your beloved pet.

A Shih Tzu has very large prominent eyes placed right in front of their precious faces. There is no long muzzle as on a Labrador or a German Shepherd Dog to protect them from hazards. Daily eye checks are of the utmost importance. Clear, wide open eyes with no discharge are correct. Any sign of cloudiness, irritation, excessive tearing or redness is cause for concern and a trip to the veterinarian. It could be an eye ulcer. Eye ulcers can occur spontaneously overnight for no apparent reason. I have seen

This is Ch. Regal's Jack N' The Box R.O.M. as an adult. Owner, Kathy Kwait.

dogs that leave home one day to go to a professional handler to be shown, and they just simply pop an eye ulcer from nerves the next day. I do not want you to think that we do nothing but medicate eyes, but I want you to be aware. This dog is your responsibility—it cannot get to the doctor by itself. An untreated eye can cause blindness. Occasionally a Shih Tzu can have eyelashes that grow inward, usually on their lower lid. Entropion, as the condition is known, can cause a constant source of irritation, and they should be carefully plucked out. It is best not to try this yourself, but to see your veterinarian.

CARE OF YOUR OLDER SHIH TZU

Shih Tzu have a life expectancy of 14 to 16 years. Everyone should remember that older dogs, like humans, can have their problems. I find that the Shih Tzu who reaches its later years is still a wonderful, vibrant, loving dog. Your veterinarian should be made aware if the dog seems at all stiff that it could be arthritis; has a cough that it could be a heart or lung problem; or has any unexplained bumps or lumps that they may need to be removed. Our Shih Tzu and our human family live in the same environment and are subject to the same hazards and pollution.

BREEDING the Shih Tzu

I would like to preface this chapter by saying that I really do not approve of pet owners and novices breeding litters of Shih Tzu. There is much to do before you even consider breeding any bitch. She should be thoroughly checked for diseases by your veterinarian—all inherited diseases as well as infections. An infection that is carried by a bitch can be passed to her puppies at the time of birth, and puppies can be lost. Serious consideration must be taken as to which stud to use. Simply looking in the newspaper or using your neighbor's dog will not do. Many times these dogs have not been tested or are not of a quality to be used for breeding. If a dog or bitch does not conform to the standard of the breed, it simply should not be used to reproduce more inferior puppies. This does not keep the breed pure and correct. It is a very serious responsibility when a litter of puppies is created. The breeder is, in essence, responsible for those puppies for the rest of their lives.

There is also the expense involved in having a litter of puppies. I know many people feel that if they buy a dog, they must breed it to make their money back. Truly, a family or a person buys a dog for companionship and love, not to become a puppy machine. If a person does a good and correct job of breeding, whelping,

Breeding Shih Tzu should be done responsibly and not for fun or profit. There is a great of expense involved.

44

and raising a litter of puppies, there is no money to be made. Most breeders are lucky if they break even.

After you are successful in finding the correct stud dog, having your veterinarian do all the testing, giving the bitch all the prenatal care (vet checks, vitamins, etc.), you still may have to face a Caesarean section. Shih Tzu puppies are very small (4 to 6 ounces at birth) and are very difficult to whelp and keep going without a very experienced eye to watch them.

Any Shih Tzu breeder will tell you that raising puppies is very rewarding, but not monetarily speaking.

Then there is all the care of the puppies after birth. Puppies need premium dog food to grow and develop correctly, and two or three trips to the veterinarian for checkups and shots. I do not let any puppies leave me until they are at least 12

A well-bred, healthy litter of puppies is something a breeder should be proud of.

weeks old. That is a lot of time and care. Think about it. If you do not or will not devote yourself to this, do not start.

CARING FOR A LITTER OF NEWBORN PUPS

Your bitch is pregnant. Usually you cannot tell by observation until about five or six weeks into gestation. You can have an ultrasound performed after 30 days, or your veterinarian can palpate, usually after three weeks, and check to see if the bitch has taken. Gestation for a litter of puppies is nine weeks or 63 days. I find that most pregnant Shih Tzu bitches have a great deal of trouble carrying puppies that long, especially if there are four or more puppies. Most of mine whelp up to a week early. They become so large that nature says it's time to get out. The poor little things can barely trundle around, and they are very uncomfortable.

During the time you are waiting for the arrival of the puppies some thought should go into a whelper. I have two aluminum whelpers that are about 2 feet wide and 4 feet long. There is a wall that divides about one-third of the space off so the mother can get off the heat and away from the puppies if she wishes. I find these whelpers very safe and secure. They also can be kept sterile, as you can clean them readily. They have a lid that can be closed completely; however, I never close it down. I prop it open and as the puppies get older I leave it open more and more, until it is completely up. My babies stay in the whelper until they have had their first shot. At that

Occasionally an entire litter or perhaps just one of a litter will need to be bottle-fed by the owner.

A newly born litter of puppies need a very safe and secure place that can easily be kept sterile.

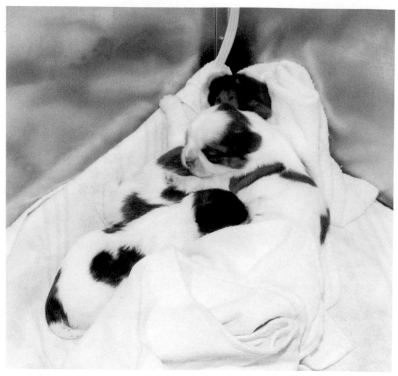

A new litter of puppies will only sleep and eat. At this age they must be kept warm.

time I put them into an ex-pen when they are not out playing. Mom will want to stay with them some part of the day, and usually all night until they are between six and seven weeks. In the beginning you will have to beg her to come out just to potty. They go nuts when you take them away from their babies. Shih Tzu are very devoted mothers and really love their babies. You certainly do not have to purchase such a whelper, but a safe, warm environment is very important to the welfare of the puppies. A cardboard box will not do. I use two double-size heating pads in the bottom of the whelper, which are wrapped with the equivalent of at least two sections of the Sunday Times. Over the heating pads I place two large bath towels folded in half. On top of that I place a bath mat topped off with a receiving blanket. They are very soft and nice for the babies to lay on. This top layer may need to be changed often, so have a good supply of bedding. I always wash all puppy bedding in bleach to avoid the possibility of germs. The temperature in the whelper should feel warm when you press the palm of your hand down on the bedding. If this is too hot the puppies will fret and crawl apart to the sides of the whelper, but they must be kept warm. It is a matter of common sense. Don't forget that they will also have the heat from their mother added to the pads. A litter of healthy puppies usually stays together and sleeps in a pile. Be aware if one separates or the mother pushes it aside— there may be a problem. Do not ignore it. There may be something wrong and nature is telling mother, but sometimes it is just the smaller one who needs a little extra help at the milk bar or to be supplemented with a bottle for a while. You can reduce the amount of heat by removing or turning off a heating pad and add more newspaper or white paper as the puppies grow. They will automatically paper train themselves. They do not want to sleep and eat in the same location in the whelper as they relieve themselves. I never take the heat completely away from the puppies until they are seven weeks and if the weather is cold there is no harm if they still want to sleep on it longer.

Most bitches will give you definite signs when they are about to whelp. Mine do not want me out of their sight. I am followed everywhere, and I mean everywhere. They will begin to nest, dig in corners, and their appetite, which up

Although at a few weeks old Shih Tzu puppies may play for short periods of time, their day is still filled with lots of naps.

This pampered pooch is owned by Kate O'Brien.

You will know when your Shih Tzu bitch is being silly or is about to whelp a litter. When about to whelp, she will begin to nest, dig in corners and lose her appetite.

until now has been voracious, suddenly seems to be non-existent. They will not be interested in dinner or a cookie. There are exceptions to the rule: some will even eat while they whelp, but most will not. Their milk will be let down anytime up to a week before they are ready to whelp. Usually when they begin their nesting, they will also begin to pant. Their contractions do not start immediately, but sometimes take up to 24 hours to begin. During this period of time, the bitch should *never* be left alone. She must be observed at all times. Once the contractions begin, a Shih Tzu bitch should not labor for more than two or three hours before she delivers a puppy. The time between puppies should never be more than two hours. If you see a green discharge before there is a puppy delivered, it means a puppy has separated from the mother. If a bitch seems to be in heavy labor and shuts down, this means that she may be in uterine inertia (her uterus has become unable to contract). If a bitch is pushing extremely hard and nothing is produced, the puppy may be too large for her to deliver or may be posterior first (breech), a very hard delivery. I have to say that if I have lost any puppies in delivery, they have usually been breech. The bitch has delivered the puppy but not the head, and by the time you can get the puppy over the ridge and the head is out the puppy is dead.

All of the above problems require immediate attention of a competent veterinarian. Hopefully your veterinarian is available to you 24 hours a day. Most Shih Tzu love to whelp their puppies in the middle of the night. You will never know how lonely it can get at three or four in the morning when you are all alone with your beloved bitch and she is in trouble. Do not hesitate, time is of the essence if you want living puppies. Many times a pit shot or a little help with moving the puppy will do, but the veterinarian has to make the decision. You should *never* give a pit shot without a veterinarian doing an internal examination first. Many times the veterinarian will take an x-ray to determine the position and number of puppies. There could be two puppies trying to get out at once, and that extra pit could spell tragedy. If the pit does not help, or the puppies are determined to be too large, the only alternative is a Caesarean section. This is usually a very safe, fast surgery. My veterinarian lives about six minutes from my home. I can count on leaving for his office, making the determination of what to do, doing the C-section and being back home within about one hour.

Now that I have given you all the horror stories, perhaps the nice normal delivery should be explained. The bitch will do it all: nesting, panting and pushing. A puppy is delivered. Immediately get a soft cloth (I use face cloths, just the right size for a puppy). Tear open the sac that encases the puppy. Hold the puppy face forward with the head tilted up but its face facing the floor. If you do not, the fluid in the sac will enter the puppy's lungs; and if you do not get it all out, the puppy will have difficulty beginning to breathe. A puppy can also develop pneumonia and die if the fluid is not removed. Once the sac is open, immediately run the cloth gently into the mouth to remove any fluid and make sure the puppy is breathing. The breathing may be shallow at first and with the mouth open but should soon slow down. Soon the mouth should close and nose breathing should begin. A puppy that gasps too long is probably in trouble. You must keep an eye on it, but you need to move on to the umbilical cord, as there could be another puppy on the way. I use hemostats (available from your veterinarian or your local pet-supply store) to clamp the cord. I place one about ¹/₂ inch from the belly of the puppy, and a second one about ¹/₂ inch from the first. Then I cut the cord between the two hemostats with a pair of not too sharp, small scissors. The scissors and the hemostats are kept in a glass of alcohol and after each delivery replaced in the alcohol. This will prevent the danger of infection. After the cord is cut, I carefully place the hemostat close to the puppy's belly, wrap the puppy in a clean face cloth and rub its back firmly but not so hard as to rub its skin off. The object of rubbing is to help the puppy breathe properly. If the puppy sounds wet or there is rattling in the chest, the puppy may need to be shaken down. To do this you hold the puppy with its head toward the floor, placing your thumb over the bridge of the nose, the first finger in the mouth, and the second finger

Helping your Shih Tzu bitch with a litter certainly is nerve wracking, however, one look at the helpless little pups makes it all worthwhile.

under the chin. This prevents the possibility of a broken neck when you shake the puppy down. Then carefully shake the puppy down with firm movements by raising the puppy to your head level and swiftly shake it toward the floor moving your arms downward. This will help remove any excess mucus or fluid from its lungs or mouth. This procedure may need to be repeated a few times over the course of the first hour or so after the puppy is born. Although it seems that this may take forever, it really only takes a matter of five minutes or so. As I said, she could immediately push out another puppy as the uterus on a bitch has two horns, and puppies are usually coming down both sides at once (they hopefully alternate coming out). You should move as quickly as possible just in case. After the puppy is nice and dry and breathing well, place it on the mother to nurse, you may have to squeeze a little milk from her teat and rub the puppy's mouth against it. Most newborns nurse readily unless they have had a hard time whelping. Keep all the puppies nursing as they are born, it stimulates labor, and also helps the mother to bond with the puppies. If she is not interested in them immediately, do not worry. She does have other things to be concerned about. Some bitches take a few

Most newborns nurse readily unless they had a hard time whelping.

hours to really
get into their
puppies. Many
of them are
simply too tired
to care. As long
as the puppies
are warm and
dry and nursing,
do not fret. Just
keep an eye on
them. I do not
like to leave a
new mother
without being
watched every few minutes for about three or four hours.

Breeders are very experienced and know exactly what needs to be done with a newborn puppy.

One more detail that will have to be taken care of after each puppy is whelped is the afterbirth. Once you have placed the puppy down you need to return to the bitch. She still has the second hemostat attached to the rest of the cord, which is in turn attached to the afterbirth. If you are very

Some Shih Tzu bitches take a few hours to really get into their puppies. Many of them are simply too tired to care.

careful and pull very gently and smoothly, you can use the hemostat to extract the afterbirth. Simply draw it slightly upward from the bitch and the afterbirth will be removed. Dispose of the afterbirth, do not allow the bitch to eat it. It gives them loose stool the next day, and you do not need that mess in your whelper. Since I started removing the afterbirths several years ago, I have found that the bitches seem to have an easier time with the next puppy. They do not have to labor to get it out and can concentrate on the puppy instead.

RAISING AN ORPHAN PUP

Occasionally there is a need to raise a puppy that has lost its mother or one that is in a litter and is so small that it cannot fend for itself. In the case of an orphan pup, you will not only have to feed it but be totally responsible for its comfort, and making sure it properly relieves itself. The mother of the litter will stimulate her puppies to urinate and defecate by gently licking them. When there is no mother, the pup must be stimulated by you. A moist cotton ball serves as the mother's tongue. The puppies will have to be relieved several times a day. They do not automatically do this when they are newborns.

Dependent puppies come in two types. The normal size puppy who for some reason needs to be fed is really a lot of fun. I use a 2-ounce nurser (available in pet-supply houses). You will get several nipples with the bottle, and must make holes of the

Puppies usually learn from their mother or from littermates. An orphan pup relies on its owner to comfort it and teach it as much as possible.

With a new Shih Tzu puppy you will have many years of fun and happiness, not to mention a few surprises.

This 10-day-old litter is owned by JoAnn Regelman.

proper size in them. In the beginning, I gently squeeze the bottle (it is plastic) to help the puppy nurse. As the puppy grows and becomes stronger, it will suck so hard that it will flatten the bottle. You may have to enlarge the holes, or use a new nipple with larger holes in it. Although some breeders prefer to tube-feed a puppy, it makes me very nervous but it can be done. I would not try to describe this procedure in a book, I believe a veterinarian should show you how. If it is not done properly, you can puncture a lung or drown the puppy in formula. I have found that a healthy puppy can be raised very well with six feedings a day. Many years ago I tried desperately to raise a litter of premature puppies, getting up every two hours during the night for two weeks. I fed them around the clock. Eventually I lost the whole litter and was devastated. I vowed never to get so involved again and decided that if they could not make it being fed between 1:00 AM and 8:00 AM, they would not make it. I have not lost one yet. They get plenty of food and thrive on this schedule.

The other type of puppy that could need your help is the smaller one in the litter or the one that gets pushed aside by the rest and needs to be supplemented. Sometimes as you observe your new litter, you will see one puppy that never seems to be nursing with the rest. This cannot go on for more than one day. You constantly put the puppy on the mother and hold it there. It starts to nurse, but as soon as you let go the mother moves or another puppy pushes it off or it simply falls off. It is just not strong enough to get its fair share. If you do not help, it will die. Again, I use the bottle method. The hole in the nipple has to be carefully adjusted so as not to drown or tire the puppy. I feed the pup every two to three hours, the same schedule as the others—no nighttime feedings. Sometimes the puppy is too small for a bottle, and I use an eyedropper to start for the first week or two. In that case, I heat the milk in a shot glass. There is no hard and fast rule about how much formula any one puppy will take. They all let you know when they have had enough. That little fat tummy is usually your first clue. I have not lost many that I hand-raised, and the ones that are hand-raised are so spoiled and people-oriented that they make the very best pets. I have saved some puppies that weighed only 2 ounces at birth. Just little strings with legs. When they make it you really feel about 20 feet tall. My

This litter of new borns will be up and about before you know it. Soon each puppy's personality will develop.

little Duncan is now 11 years old, weighs 5 pounds and rules my house. He has never had a haircut, runs around the kitchen demanding everyone's attention, has to be the first one to the door, and has the biggest mouth in the house. He is so spoiled, and still thinks I am his mother. I call him my "rug rat."

I use a formula that I received from a veterinarian who told me that it was the one used in the zoo in Philadelphia. He worked there as a student while at the University of Pennsylvania. Evidently all the veterinary students spent time at the zoo. This formula has stood me well for 20 years. I have only one reservation each time I've made it recently, and that is the problem we now have with raw eggs, but the puppies seem to thrive on it, so I have not given up using it. The formula is as follows:

1 egg yolk (Make sure there is no white. Puppies cannot digest the white.)

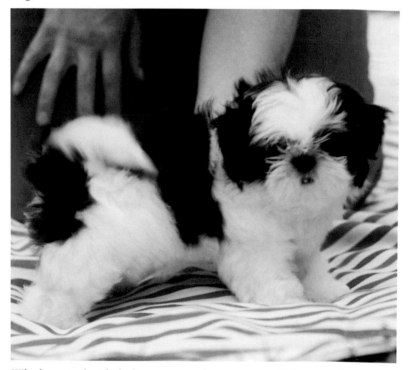

Whether raised with the litter or an orphan pup, you will be sure to have a most enjoyable pet with a Shih Tzu.

Good nutrition will help your puppy grow to it fullest potential

1 cup of whole milk
1 teaspoon of lactose (milk sugar) (Get from pharmacy.)
1 teaspoon of lime water (Get from pharmacy.)

I put all the ingredients in a two-cup shaker with a pour top and shake well. Keep refrigerated at all times. Shake well before you put into bottle to heat (the formula should never be heated more than twice). Throw it out if unused. Do not take a chance on making the puppy sick. If a large quantity of formula is not used up in two to three days, I dispose of it and make new. The bottle can be heated in a large cup of hot water or placed in the microwave for a few seconds. Keep the bottle scrupulously clean. Sour milk will really upset the babies, not to mention the germs that could grow.

There are also several brands of formula on the market that you can use. Consult your veterinarian.

SHOWING Your Shih Tzu

Choosing a "show dog" is not something to be taken lightly or on the spur of the moment. Once you have contracted with a breeder to become the owner and caretaker of a very special puppy deemed the quality to be in the show ring, you must follow through with this commitment. It is very difficult for most ethical breeders to part with that special puppy. In my case I have been working for 20 years to create what, in my mind and eyes, is a Shih Tzu that is correct and to the standard. It is heartbreaking for the breeder to entrust their puppy to someone who says they will follow all the breeder's instructions and then allows the dog to be wasted and never make the show ring. It takes me a long time to decide that a novice or newcomer to me is going to make an appropriate home for my dog. The life of a show dog is in many ways quite different from that of your pet. Shih Tzu, being a coated breed, have all that wonderful hair. It has been the downfall of many a great dog. They have a good body and a wonderful temperament for the show ring, but that coat can get the best of the owner. If the dog is not "in coat," they cannot compete in the ring today. Grooming has become a very important part of this breed. I am not saying that I totally approve of this, but it is the truth: The glamour seems sometimes to count more than soundness.

The standard for our breed, which has been determined by the Board of the American Shih Tzu Club, Inc. and the approximately 700 people who belong to the Club, is very demanding. A dog who does not conform to the standard in most ways (there is no such thing as a perfect dog) should not be shown to championship or used in anyone's breeding program. A dog that is going to be used in this manner should also be tested very carefully for inherited and genetic faults. Any serious health problems should automatically exclude any dog from the show ring, as most show dogs end up in someone's breeding program, therefore passing on their faults.

Ch. Ultra's Guilty As Sin "Felon," owned by Eileen Nicholas.

A champion Shih Tzu is one that conforms to the standard in most ways.

Now your job of raising your Shih Tzu to be happy and ring-ready begins. This means socialization, match shows, grooming, stacking on a grooming table and the ground, moving correctly in the ring, and generally behaving in the show environment.

You start with the best food available so your puppy grows up well-nourished, well-bodied, and with a very healthy coat. A show Shih Tzu needs to be brushed daily, bathed weekly, and when it reaches the age of six to eight months should be kept in an ex-pen to protect the coat. As I said before, coat should not determine who wins, but many times it is a determining factor. The owner should take the puppy to "match shows" and handling classes so that they both learn the ins and outs of the show ring. I can remember standing in the ring at the table literally shaking in my boots

There is nothing more gratifying than going to a dog show, grooming your dog, and entering the ring with competitors.

when I first started showing my dogs. You have to learn to become more confident as your nerves can very easily transfer to the dog, and you will both be a wreck in the ring. Ring presence for you and your dog will come with experience: it really cannot be taught; it has to be acquired.

There is nothing more gratifying than going to a dog show, grooming out your dog, and entering the ring with competitors, then standing in first place with that blue ribbon in your hands. It really can be a thrill, you are so proud of your dog at that moment, and should be proud of yourself to have gotten that far. In this breed many breeders opt to use professional handlers. The dog goes to live with the handler for a period of time, the handler takes over complete care and grooming of the dog, makes the entries for the dog shows, shows your dog, and hopefully wins. The owner waits at home on the weekend for that phone call, or if they are lucky enough that the show is close to home they can go to the show to watch their dog.

The Shih Tzu standard states that its coat is long and flowing, as this new champion clearly shows.

The Shih Tzu's Chinese ancestry as a highly valued and palace pet shines through to today's Shih Tzu owners, especially those of the show world.

My best advice to a novice that is considering a show dog in their life is to find a reliable, ethical breeder to help you through your first show dogs and go have fun. There is really too much that goes into a *champion* for me to put down here in writing.

Here is a description of the ideal Shih Tzu as approved by the American Kennel Club. The England standard follows as it is quite different and is helpful to compare the divergence in type from British to America.

AKC STANDARD FOR THE SHIH TZU

General Appearance—The Shih Tzu is a sturdy, lively, alert Toy dog with long flowing double coat. Befitting his noble Chinese ancestry as a highly valued, prize companion and palace pet, the Shih Tzu is proud of bearing, has a distinctively arrogant carriage with head well up and tail curved over the back. Although there has always been considerable size variation, the Shih Tzu must be compact, solid, carrying good weight and substance. Even though a Toy dog, the Shih Tzu must be subject to the same requirements of soundness and structure prescribed for all breeds, and any deviation from the ideal described in the standard should be penalized to the extent of deviation.

Structural faults common to all breeds are as undesirable in the Shih Tzu as in any other breed.

Size, Proportion, Substance—*Size*—Ideally, height at withers is 9 to 10.5 inches; but no less than 8 inches nor more than 11 inches. Ideally, weight of mature dogs, 9 to 16 pounds. *Proportion*—Length between withers and root of tail is slightly longer than height at withers. *The Shih Tzu must never be so high stationed as to appear leggy nor so low stationed as to appear dumpy or squatty. Substance*—Regardless of size, the Shih Tzu is *always* compact, solid and carries good weight and substance.

Head—*Head*—Round, broad, wide between eyes, its size *in balance* with the overall size of dog being neither too large or too small. *Fault*: Narrow head, close-set eyes. *Expression*—Warm, sweet, wide-eyed, friendly and trusting. An overall well-balanced and pleasant expression supercedes the importance of individual parts. *Care should be taken to look and examine well beyond the hair to determine if what is seen is the actual head and expression rather than an image created by grooming technique. Eyes*—Large, round, not prominent, placed well apart, looking straight ahead. *Very dark*. Lighter on liver pigmented dogs and blue pigmented dogs. *Fault*: Small; close set or light eyes; excessive eye whites. *Ears*—Large, set slightly below crown of skull; heavily coated. *Skull*—Domed. *Stop*—There is a *definite stop*. *Muzzle*—Square, short, unwrinkled with good cushioning, set no

At a conformation show, a judge takes all aspects of the standard into consideration for each and every dog.

The Shih Tzu's expression is always warm, sweet, wide-eyed, friendly and trusting.

Ch. Regel's Kaluha and Cream owned by JoAnn Regelman.

lower than bottom eye rim; never downturned. Ideally, no longer than one inch from tip of nose to stop, although length may vary slightly in relation to overall size of dog. Front of muzzle should be flat; lower lip and chin not protruding and definitely never receding. *Fault*: Snipiness, lack of definite stop. *Nose*—Nostrils are broad, wide, and open. *Pigmentation*—Nose, lips, eye rims are black on all colors, except liver on liver pigmented dogs and blue on blue pigmented dogs. *Fault*: Pink on nose, lips, or eye rims. *Bite*—Undershot. Jaw is not broad and wide. A missing tooth or slightly misaligned teeth should not be too severely penalized. Teeth and tongue should not show when mouth is closed. *Fault*: Overshot bite.

Neck, Topline, Body—*Of utmost importance is an overall well-balanced dog with no exaggerated features. Neck*—Well set-on flowing smoothly into shoulders; of sufficient length to permit natural high head carriage and in balance with height and length of dog. *Topline*—Level. *Body*—Short-coupled and sturdy with no waist or tuck-up. The Shih Tzu is slightly longer than tall. *Fault*: Legginess. *Chest*—Broad and deep with good spring of rib, however, not barrel-chested. Depth of rib cage should extend to just below elbow. Distance from elbow to withers is a little greater than from elbow to ground. *Croup*—Flat. *Tail*—Set on high, heavily plumed, carried in curve well over back. Too loose, too tight, too flat, or too low set a tail is undesirable and should be penalized to the extent of deviation.

Forequarters—*Shoulders*—Well angulated, well laid back, well laid-in, fitting smoothly into body. *Legs*—Straight, well-boned, muscular, set well-apart and under chest, with elbows set close to body. *Pasterns*—strong, perpendicular. *Dewclaws*—May be removed. *Feet*—Firm, well padded, point straight ahead.

Hindquarters—*Angulation of hindquarters should be in balance with forequarters. Legs*—Well-boned, muscular, and

Ch. Regel's Stuffed Teddi winning Group 3 at the Hanover Kennel Club. Owned by JoAnn Regelman.

Ch. Regel's The Proof Is N' The Puddin owned by JoAnn Regelman.

straight when viewed from rear with well-bent stifles, not close set but in line with forequarters. **Hocks**—well let down, perpendicular. **Fault**: Hyperextension of hocks. **Dewclaws**—May be removed. **Feet**—Firm, well-padded, pointed straight ahead.

Coat—Luxurious, double-coated, dense, long and flowing. Slight wave permissible. Hair on top of head is tied up. **Fault**: Sparse coat, single coat, curly coat. **Trimming**—Feet, bottom of coat, and anus may be done for neatness and to facilitate movement. **Fault**: Excessive trimming.

Color and Markings—*All* are permissible and to be considered *equally*.

Gait—The Shih Tzu moves straight and must be shown at its natural speed, *neither raced nor strung-up*, to evaluate its smooth, flowing, effortless movement with good front reach and equally strong rear drive, level topline, naturally high head carriage, and tail carried in gentle curve over back.

Temperament—As the sole purpose of the Shih Tzu is that of a companion and house pet, it is essential that its temperament be outgoing, happy, affectionate, friendly and trusting toward all.

Kennel Club Standard for the Shih Tzu

General Appearance: Sturdy, abundantly coated dog with distinctly arrogant carriage and chrysanthemum-like face.

Characteristics: Intelligent, active and alert.

Head and Skull: Head broad, round, wide between eyes. Shock-headed with hair falling well over eyes. Good beard and whiskers, hair growing upwards on the nose giving a distinctive chrysanthemum-like effect. Muzzle of ample width, square, short, not wrinkled; flat and hairy. Nose black but dark liver in liver-marked dogs and about one inch from tip of definite stop. Nose level or slightly tip-titled. Top of nose leather should be on a line with or slightly below lower eyerim. Wide-open nostrils. Downpointed nose highly undesirable, as are pinched nostrils. Pigmentation of muzzle as unbroken as possible.

Eyes: Large, dark, round, placed well apart but not prominent. Warm expression. In liver or liver-marked dogs, lighter eye colour permissible. No white of eye showing.

The Shih Tzu of Great Britain clearly differs in appearance from the Shih Tzu of the US.

Ears: Large, with long leathers, carried drooping, Set slightly below crown of skull, so heavily coated they appear to blend into hair of neck.

Mouth: Wide, slightly undershot or level. Lips level.

Neck: Well proportioned, nicely arched. Sufficient length to carry head proudly.

Forequarters: Shoulders well laid back. Legs short and muscular with ample bone, as straight as possible, consistent with broad chest being well let down.

Body: Longer between withers and root of tail than height of withers, well coupled and sturdy, chest broad and deep, shoulders firm, back level.

Hindquarters: Legs short and muscular with ample bone. Straight when viewed from the rear. Thighs well rounded and muscular. Legs looking massive on account of wealth of hair.

Feet: Rounded, firm and well padded, appearing big on account of wealth of hair.

Tail: Heavily plumed, carried gaily well over back. Set on high. Height approximately level with that of skull to give a balanced outline.

Gait/Movement: Arrogant, smooth-flowing, front legs reaching well forward, strong rear action and showing full pad.

Coat: Long, dense, not curly, with good undercoat. Slight wave permitted. Strongly recommended that hair on head tied up.

Colour: All colours permissible, white blaze on forehead and white tip to tail highly desirable in parti-colours.

Size: Height at withers not more than 26.7 cm (10 in), type and breed character-istics of the utmost importance and on no account to be sacrificed to size alone. Weight: 4.5-8.1 kgs (10-18 lbs). Ideal

Ch. Regel's Elusive Danny Boy R.O.M. Owned by JoAnn Regelman.

weight: 4.5-7.3 kgs (10-16 lbs).

Faults: Any departure from the foregoing points should be considered a fault and the seriousness with which the fault should be regarded should be in exact proportion to its degree.

Note: Male animals should have two apparently normal testicles fully descended into the scrotum.

CONFORMATION

Conformation showing is our oldest dog show sport. This

Prior to six months of age you may show in puppy matches to get your Shih Tzu acquainted with the ring procedures.

type of showing is based on the dog's appearance—that is his structure, movement and attitude. When considering this type of showing, you need to be aware of your breed's standard and be able to evaluate your dog compared to that standard. The breeder of your puppy or other experienced breeders would be good sources for such an evaluation. Puppies can go through lots of changes over a period of time. I always say most puppies start out as promising hopefuls and then after maturing may be disappointing as show candidates. Even so this should not deter them from being excellent pets.

Usually conformation training classes are offered by the local kennel or obedience clubs. These are excellent places for training puppies. The puppy should be able to walk on a lead before entering such a class. Proper ring procedure and technique for posing (stacking) the dog will be demonstrated as well as gaiting the dog. Usually certain patterns are used in the ring such as the triangle or the "L." Conformation class, like the PKT class, will give your youngster the opportunity to socialize with different breeds of dogs and humans too.

It takes some time to learn the routine of conformation show-ing. Usually one starts at the puppy matches which may be AKC Sanctioned or Fun Matches. These matches are generally for puppies from two or three months to a year old, and there may be classes for the adult over the age of 12 months. Similar to point shows, the classes are divided by sex and after completion of the classes in that breed or variety, the class winners compete for Best of Breed or

SHIH TZU FANCIERS
OF GREATER BALTIMORE

FIRST

12 TO 18

IN SWEEPSTAKES

To compete in the dog show world requires dedication, hard work and a lot of long hours.

Qualifying for a championship is based on a point system. These points are given in accordance with a scale of points established by the AKC.

Variety. The winner goes on to compete in the Group and the Group winners compete for Best in Match. No championship points are awarded for match wins.

A few matches can be great training for puppies even though there is no intention to go on showing. Matches enable the puppy to meet new people and be handled by a stranger—the judge. It is also a change of environment, which broadens the horizon for both dog and handler. Matches and other dog activities boost the confidence of the handler and especially the younger handlers.

Earning an AKC championship is built on a point system, which is different from Great Britain. To become an AKC Champion of Record the dog must earn 15 points. The number of points earned each time depends upon the number of dogs in competition. The number of points available at each show depends upon the breed, its sex and the location of the show. The United States is divided into ten AKC zones. Each zone has its own set of points. The purpose of the zones is to try to equalize the points available from breed to breed and area to area. The AKC adjusts the point scale annually.

This is Ch. Tu Chu Munchkintown Art Deco R.O.M. owned by Kathy Kwait.

The number of points that can be won at a show are between one and five. Three-, four- and five-point wins are considered majors. Not only does the dog need 15 points won under three different judges, but those points must include two majors under two different judges. Canada also works on a point system but majors are not required.

Dogs always show before bitches. The classes available to those seeking points are: Puppy (which may be divided into 6 to 9 months and 9 to 12 months); 12 to 18 months; Novice; Bred-by-Exhibitor; American-bred; and Open. The class winners of the same sex of each breed or variety compete against each other for Winners Dog and Winners Bitch. A Reserve Winners Dog and Reserve Winners Bitch are also awarded but do not carry any points unless the Winners win is disallowed by AKC. The Winners Dog and Bitch compete with the specials (those dogs that have attained championship) for Best of Breed or Variety, Best of Winners and Best of Opposite Sex. It is possible to pick up an extra point or even a major if the points are higher for the defeated winner than those of Best of Winners. The latter would get the higher total from the defeated winner.

At an all-breed show, each Best of Breed or Variety winner will go on to his respective Group and then the Group

These two beauties are Jennylyn Aslan Anne and Jennylyn Sun Bonnet owned by Debra Emerson and Jennifer Lynn Winship.

winners will compete against each other for Best in Show. There are seven Groups: Sporting, Hounds, Working, Terriers, Toys, Non-Sporting and Herding. Obviously there are no Groups at speciality shows (those shows that have only one breed or a show such as the American Spaniel Club's Flushing Spaniel Show, which is for all flushing spaniel breeds).

Earning a championship in England is somewhat different since they do not have a point system. Challenge Certificates are awarded if the judge feels the dog is deserving regardless of the number of dogs in competition. A dog must earn three Challenge Certificates under three different judges, with at least one of these Certificates being won after the age of 12 months. Competition is very strong and entries may be higher than they are in the U.S. The Kennel Club's Challenge Certificates are only available at Championship Shows.

In England, The Kennel Club regulations require that certain dogs, Border Collies and Gundog breeds, qualify in a working capacity (i.e., obedience or field trials) before becoming a full Champion. If they do not qualify in the working aspect, then they are designated a Show Champion, which is equivalent to the AKC's Champion of Record. A Gundog may be granted the title of Field Trial Champion (FT Ch) if it passes all the tests in the field but would also have to qualify in conformation before becoming a full Champion. A Border Collie that earns the title of Obedience

Westminster Kennel Club 1996 in New York. This is the American Kennel Club's most prestigious show.

1996 Westminster Kennel Club Best of Breed Winner Ch. Symarun's Romeo At Hidden Key owned by Linda and Roy Ward.

Champion (Ob Ch) must also qualify in the conformation ring before becoming a Champion.

The U.S. doesn't have a designation full Champion but does award for Dual and Triple Champions. The Dual Champion must be a Champion of Record, and either Champion Tracker, Herding Champion, Obedience Trial Champion or Field Champion. Any dog that has been awarded the titles of Champion of Record, and any two of the following: Champion Tracker, Herding Champion, Obedience Trial Champion or Field Champion, may be designated as a Triple Champion.

The shows in England seem to put more emphasis on breeder judges than those in the U.S. There is much competition within the breeds. Therefore the quality of the individual breeds should be very good. In the United States we tend to have more "all around judges" (those that judge multiple breeds) and use the breeder judges at the specialty shows. Breeder judges are more familiar with their own breed since they are actively breeding that breed or did so at one time. Americans emphasize Group and Best in Show wins and promote them accordingly.

It is my understanding that the shows in England can be very large and extend over several days, with the Groups being scheduled on different days. I believe there is only one all-breed show in the U.S. that extends over two days, the Westminster Kennel Club Show. In our country we have cluster shows, where several different clubs will use the same show site over consecutive days.

Westminster Kennel Club is our most prestigious show although the entry is limited to 2500. In recent years, entry has been limited to Champions. This show is more formal than the major-

ity of the shows with the judges wearing formal attire and the handlers fashionably dressed. In most in-stances the quality of the dogs is superb. After all, it is a show of Champions. It is a good

Aside from the dazzling trophies it awards, dog showing is rewarding in many ways for both owner and dog.

82

show to study the AKC registered breeds and is by far the most exciting—especially since it is televised! WKC is one of the few shows in this country that is still benched. This means the dog must be in his benched area during the show hours except when he is being groomed, in the ring, or being exercised.

If you are handling your own dog, please give some consideration to your apparel. For sure the dress

Crufts dog show is England's prestigious show. Handlers and their dogs have a large competition field, nearly 20,000.

code at matches is more informal than the point shows. However, you should wear something a little more appropriate than beach attire or ragged jeans and bare feet. If you check out the handlers and see what is presently fashionable, you'll catch on. Men usually dress with a shirt and tie and a nice sports coat. Whether you are male or female, you will want to wear comfortable

Obedience trials traditionally attract sporting breeds, though toy breeds can excel as well.

clothes and shoes. You need to be able to run with your dog and you certainly don't want to take a chance of falling and hurting yourself. Heaven forbid, if nothing else, you'll upset your dog. Women usually wear a dress or two-piece outfit, preferably with pockets to carry bait, comb, brush, etc. In this case men are the lucky ones with all their pockets. Ladies, think about where your dress will be if you need to kneel on the floor and also think about running. Does it allow freedom to do so?

Years ago, after toting around all the baby paraphernalia, I found toting the dog and necessities a breeze. You need to take

Lady handlers should wear comfortable clothing that allows them freedom to move and that does not distract from the dog.

along dog; crate; ex pen (if you use one); extra newspaper; water pail and water; all required grooming equipment, including hair dryer and extension cord; table; chair for you; bait for dog and lunch for you and friends; and, last but not least, clean up materials, such as plastic bags, paper towels, and perhaps a bath towel and some shampoo—just in case. Don't forget your entry confirmation and directions to the show.

Clothing that contains pockets is most useful to carry extra bait as well as a brush or comb.

If you are showing in obedience, then you will want to wear pants. Many of our top obedience handlers wear pants that are color-coordinated with their dogs. The philosophy is that imperfections in the black dog will be less obvious next to your black pants.

Whether you are showing in conformation, Junior Showmanship or obedience, you need to watch the clock and be sure you are not late. It is customary to pick up your conformation armband a few minutes before the start of the class. They will not wait for you and if you are on the show grounds and not in the ring, you will upset everyone. It's a little more complicated picking up your obedience armband if you show later in the class. If you have not picked up your armband and they get to your number, you may not be allowed to show. It's best to pick up your armband early, but then you may show earlier than expected if other handlers don't pick up. Customarily all conflicts should be discussed with the judge prior to the start of the class.

Junior Showmanship

The Junior Showmanship Class is a wonderful way to build self confidence even if there are no aspirations of staying with the dog-show game later in life. Frequently, Junior Showmanship becomes the background of those who become successful exhibitors/handlers in the future. In some instances it is taken very seriously, and success is measured in terms of wins. The Junior Handler is judged solely on his ability and skill in presenting his dog. The dog's conformation is not to be considered by the judge. Even so the condition and grooming of the dog may be a reflection upon the handler.

Usually the matches and point shows include different classes. The Junior Handler's dog may be entered in a breed or obedience class and even shown by another person in that class. Junior Showmanship classes are usually divided by age and perhaps sex. The age is determined by the handler's age on the day of the show. The classes are:

Novice Junior for those at least ten and under 14 years of age who at time of entry closing have not won three first places in a Novice Class at a licensed or member show.

Novice Senior for those at least 14 and under 18 years of age who at the time of entry closing have not won three first places in a Novice Class at a licensed or member show.

Open Junior for those at least ten and under 14 years of age who at the time of entry closing have won at least three first

Am. Mex. Int. Ch. Loubren's Ninja Star R.O.M. owned by Earl and Xena Takahashi of Xeralane Shih Tzu is a perfect example of a true tri-color.

A show dog is born with a degree of physical perfection that closely approximates the standard by which the breed is judged in the ring.

places in a Novice Junior Showmanship Class at a licensed or member show with competition present.

Open Senior for those at least 14 and under 18 years of age who at time of entry closing have won at least three first places in a Novice Junior Showmanship Class at a licensed or member show with competition present.

Junior Handlers must include their AKC Junior Handler number on each show entry. This needs to be obtained from the AKC.

BEHAVIOR and Canine Communication

Studies of the human/animal bond point out the importance of the unique relationships that exist between people and their pets. Those of us who share our lives with pets understand the special part they play through companionship, service and protection.

Senior citizens show more concern for their own eating habits when they have the responsibility of feeding a dog. Seeing that their dog is routinely exercised encourages the owner to think of schedules that otherwise may seem unimportant to the senior citizen. The older owner may be arthritic and feeling poorly but with responsibility for his dog he has a reason to get up and get moving. It is a big plus if his dog is an attention seeker who will demand such from his owner.

Over the last couple of decades, it has been shown that pets relieve the stress of those who lead busy lives. Owning a pet has been known to lessen the occurrence of heart attack and stroke.

Many single folks thrive on the companionship of a dog. Lifestyles are very different from a long time ago, and today more individuals seek

In today's hectic world a companion dog has proven to reduce stress. Two Shih Tzu would prove very relaxing!

the single life. However, they receive ful-fillment from owning a dog.

Most likely the majority of our dogs live in family environments. The companionship they provide is well worth the effort involved. In my opinion, every child should have the opportunity to have a

This is Ch. Regel's Poppin Fresh all dressed up and waiting to show. Owned by JoAnn Regelman.

family dog. Dogs teach responsibility through understanding their care, feelings and even respecting their life cycles. Frequently those children who have not been exposed to dogs grow up afraid of dogs, which isn't good. Dogs sense timidity and some will take advantage of the situation.

Although it cannot speak, your pet Shih Tzu will somehow be able to understand your moods.

A Shih Tzu puppy will require extra nap times, but after that he will be at your service and ready to play!

Today more dogs are serving as service dogs. Since the origination of the Seeing Eye dogs years ago, we now have trained hearing dogs. Also dogs are trained to provide service for the handicapped and are able to perform many different tasks for their owners. Search and Rescue dogs, with their handlers, are sent throughout the world to assist in recovery of disaster victims. They are life savers.

Therapy dogs are very popular with nursing homes, and some hospitals even allow them to visit. The inhabitants truly look forward to their visits. I have taken a couple of my dogs visiting and left in tears when I saw the response of the patients. They wanted and were allowed to have my dogs in their beds to hold and love.

Nationally there is a Pet Awareness Week to educate students and others about the value and basic care of our pets. Many countries take an even greater interest in their pets than Americans do. In those countries the pets are allowed to accompany their owners into restaurants and shops, etc. In the U.S. this freedom is only available to our service dogs. Even so we think very highly of the human/animal bond.

CANINE BEHAVIOR

Canine behavior problems are the number-one reason for pet owners to dispose of their dogs, either through new homes, humane shelters or euthanasia. Unfortunately there are too many owners who are unwilling to devote the necessary time to properly train their dogs. On the other hand, there are those who not only are concerned about inherited health problems but are also aware of the dog's mental stability.

You may realize that a breed and his group relatives (i.e., sporting, hounds, etc.) show tendencies to behavioral characteristics.

This is "Scarlet", owned by Dee Shepherd, all done up for Halloween in her Lion Suit.

An experienced breeder can acquaint you with his breed's personality. Unfortunately many breeds are labeled with poor temperaments when actually the breed as a whole is not affected but only a small percentage of individuals within the breed.

If the breed in question is very popular, then of course there may be a higher number of unstable dogs. Do not label a breed good or bad. I know of absolutely awful-tempered dogs within one of our most popular, lovable breeds.

Inheritance and environment contribute to the dog's behavior. Some naïve people suggest inbreeding as the cause of bad temperaments. Inbreeding only results in poor behavior if the ancestors carry the trait. If there are excellent temperaments behind the dogs, then inbreeding will promote good temperaments in the offspring. Did you ever consider that inbreeding is what sets the characteristics of a breed? A purebred dog is the end result of inbreeding. This does not spare the mixed-breed dog from the same problems. Mixed-breed dogs frequently are the offspring of purebred dogs.

When planning a breeding, I like to observe the potential stud and his offspring in the show ring. If I see unruly behavior, I try to look into it further. I want to know if it is genetic or environmental, due to the lack of training and socialization. A good breeder will avoid breeding mentally unsound dogs.

Not too many decades ago most of our dogs led a different lifestyle than what is prevalent today. Usually mom stayed home so

the dog had human companionship and someone to discipline it if needed. Not much was expected from the dog. Today's mom works and everyone's life is at a much faster pace.

The dog may have to adjust to being a "weekend" dog. The family is gone all day during

Some Shih Tzu will sleep all day while their family is away, however, others will lead an active and perhaps glamorous lifestyle.

Shih Tzu have excellent temperaments and are very agreeable dogs. With patience and love they can be trained to do just about anything.

The Shih Tzu's small size and easy going personality make it a wonderful house dog, but it still should have regular periods of exercise to keep up its good health.

the week, and the dog is left to his own devices for entertainment. Some dogs sleep all day waiting for their family to come home and others become wigwam wreckers if given the opportunity. Crates do ensure the safety of the dog and the house. However, he could become a physically and emotionally cripple if he doesn't get enough exercise and attention. We still appreciate and want the companionship of our dogs although we expect more from them. In many cases we tend to forget dogs are just that—*dogs* not human beings.

I own several dogs who are left crated during the day but I do try to make time for them in the evenings and on the weekends. Also we try to do something together before I leave for work. Maybe it helps them to have the companionship of other dogs. They accept their crates as their personal "houses" and seem to be content with their routine and thrive on trying their best to please me.

Socializing and Training

Many prospective puppy buyers lack experience regarding the proper socialization and training needed to develop the type of pet we all desire. In the first 18 months, training does take some work. Trust me, it is easier to start proper training before there is a problem that needs to be corrected.

The initial work begins with the breeder. The breeder should start socializing the puppy at five to six weeks of age and cannot let up. Human socializing is critical up through 12 weeks of age and likewise important during the following months. The litter should be left together during the first few weeks but it is necessary to separate them by ten weeks of age. Leaving them together after that time will increase competition for litter dominance. If puppies are not socialized with people by 12 weeks of age, they will be timid in later life.

The eight- to ten-week age period is a fearful time for puppies. They need to be handled very gently around children and adults.

Training your Shih Tzu will ensure that you have a well mannered housedog and companion.

Exercise pens are great ways to allow your Shih Tzu outside, however, still have him confined.

There should be no harsh discipline during this time. Starting at 14 weeks of age, the puppy begins the juvenile period, which ends when he reaches sexual maturity around six to 14 months of age. During the juvenile period he needs to be introduced to strangers (adults, children and other dogs) on the home property. At sexual maturity he will begin to bark at strangers and become more protective. Males start to lift their legs to urinate but if you desire you can inhibit this behavior by walking your boy on leash away from trees, shrubs, fences, etc.

Your Shih Tzu should be meet as many strangers and be placed in as many different situations as possible to avoid an unsociable pet.

Perhaps you are thinking about an older puppy. You need to inquire about the puppy's social experience. If he has lived in a kennel, he may have a hard time adjusting to people and environmental stimuli. Assuming he has had a good social upbringing, there are advantages to an older puppy.

Training includes puppy kindergarten and a minimum of one to two basic training classes. During these classes you will learn how to dominate your youngster. This is especially important if you own a large breed of dog. It is somewhat harder, if not nearly impossible, for some owners to be the Alpha figure when their dog towers over them. You will be taught how to properly restrain your dog. This concept is important. Again it puts you in the Alpha position. All dogs need to be restrained many times during their lives. Believe it or not, some of our worst offenders are the eight-week-old puppies that are brought to our clinic. They need to be gently restrained for a nail trim but the way they carry on you would think we were killing them. In comparison, their vaccination is a "piece of cake." When we ask dogs to do something that is not agreeable to them, then their worst comes out. Life will be easier for your dog if you expose him at a young age to the necessities of life—proper behavior and restraint.

UNDERSTANDING THE DOG'S LANGUAGE

Most authorities agree that the dog is a descendent of the wolf. The dog and wolf have similar traits. For instance both are pack oriented and prefer not to be isolated for long periods of time. Another characteristic is that the dog, like the wolf, looks to the leader—Alpha—for direction. Both the wolf and the dog communicate through body language, not only within their pack but with outsiders.

Every pack has an Alpha figure. The dog looks to you, or should look to you, to be that leader. If your dog doesn't receive the proper training and guidance, he very well may replace you as Alpha. This would be a serious problem and is certainly a disservice to your dog.

Eye contact is one way the Alpha wolf keeps order within his pack. You are Alpha so you must establish eye contact with your puppy. Obviously your puppy will have to look at you. Practice eye contact even if you need to hold his head for five to ten seconds at a time. You can give him a treat as a reward. Make sure your eye contact is gentle and not threatening. Later, if he has been naughty, it is permissible to give him a long, penetrating look. I caution you there are some older dogs that never learned eye contact as puppies and cannot accept eye contact. You should avoid eye contact with these dogs since they feel threatened and will retaliate as such.

Certain rules should be laid down in the home and consistently kept. You cannot allow your Shih Tzu on the sofa one day and then expect him to stay off the next.

Body Language

The play bow, when the forequarters are down and the hindquarters are elevated, is an invitation to play. Puppies play fight, which helps them learn the acceptable limits of biting. This is necessary for later in their lives. Nevertheless, an owner may be falsely reassured by the playful nature of his dog's aggression. Playful aggression toward another dog or human may be an indication of serious aggression in

Making eye contact with your Shih Tzu is very important if you want him to listen to you.

the future. Owners should never play fight or play tug-of-war with any dog that is inclined to be dominant.

Signs of submission are:
1. Avoids eye contact.
2. Active submission—the dog crouches down, ears back and the tail is lowered.
3. Passive submission—the dog rolls on his side with his hindlegs in the air and frequently urinates.

Signs of dominance are:
1. Makes eye contact.
2. Stands with ears up, tail up and the hair raised on his neck.
3. Shows dominance over another dog by standing at right angles over it.

Dominant dogs tend to behave in characteristic ways such as:
1. The dog may be unwilling to move from his place (i.e., reluctant to give up the sofa if the owner wants to sit there).
2. He may not part with toys or objects in his mouth and may show possessiveness with his food bowl.
3. He may not respond quickly to commands.

4. He may be disagreeable for grooming and dislikes to be petted.

Dogs are popular because of their sociable nature. Those that have contact with humans during the first 12 weeks of life regard them as a member of their own species—their pack. All dogs have the potential for both dominant and submissive behavior. Only through experience and training do they learn to whom it is appropriate to show which behavior. Not all dogs are concerned with dominance but owners need to be aware of that potential. It is wise for the owner to establish his dominance early on.

A human can express dominance or submission toward a dog in the following ways:

1. Meeting the dog's gaze signals dominance. Averting the gaze signals submission. If the dog growls or threatens, averting the gaze is the first avoiding action to take—it may prevent attack. It is important to establish eye contact in the puppy. The older dog that has not been exposed to eye contact may see it as a threat and will not be willing to submit.

2. Being taller than the dog signals dominance; being lower signals submission. This is why, when attempting to make friends with a strange dog or catch the runaway, one should kneel down to his level. Some owners see their dogs become dominant when allowed on the furniture or on the bed. Then he is at the owner's level.

3. An owner can gain dominance by ignoring all the dog's social

When you want your Shih Tzu to do something you must be firm and consistent. Never treat your dog harshly, but never give in either.

Your little Shih Tzu will always look to you for love and companionship.

Most Shih Tzu owners try to make their little pets as comfortable as possible.

initiatives. The owner pays attention to the dog only when he obeys a command.

No dog should be allowed to achieve dominant status over any adult or child. Ways of preventing are as follows:

1. Handle the puppy gently, especially during the three- to four-month period.
2. Let the children and adults handfeed him and teach him to take food without lunging or grabbing.
3. Do not allow him to chase children or joggers.
4. Do not allow him to jump on people or mount their legs. Even females may be inclined to mount. It is not only a male habit.
5. Do not allow him to growl for any reason.
6. Don't participate in wrestling or tug-of-war games.
7. Don't physically punish puppies for aggressive behavior. Restrain him from repeating the infraction and teach an alternative

behavior. Dogs should earn everything they receive from their owners. This would include sitting to receive petting or treats, sitting before going out the door and sitting to receive the collar and leash. These types of exercises reinforce the owner's dominance.

Young children should never be left alone with a dog. It is important that children learn some basic obedience commands so they have some control over the dog. They will gain the respect of their dog.

FEAR

One of the most common problems dogs experience is being fearful. Some dogs are more afraid than others. On the lesser side, which is sometimes humorous to watch, my dog can be afraid of a strange object. He acts silly when something is out of place in the house. I call his problem perceptive intelligence. He realizes the abnormal within his known environment. He does not react the same way in strange environments since he does not know what is normal.

On the more serious side is a fear of people. This can result in backing off, seeking his own space and saying "leave me alone" or it can result in an aggressive behavior that may lead to challenging the person. Respect that the dog that

Shih Tzu, like all dogs should earn everything they receive from their owners. Make it sit, lay down or go to its bed before you reward it with a toy or snack.

wants to be left alone and give him time to come forward. If you approach the cornered dog, he may resort to snapping. If you leave him alone, he may decide to come forward, which should be rewarded with a treat. Years ago we had a dog that behaved in this manner. We coaxed people to stop by the house and make friends with our fearful dog. She learned to take the treats and after weeks of work she overcame her suspicions and made friends more readily.

Some dogs may initially be too fearful to take treats. In these cases it is helpful to make sure the dog hasn't eaten for about 24 hours. Being a little hungry encourages him to accept the treats, especially if they are of the "gourmet" variety. I have a dog that worries about strangers since people seldom stop by my house. Over the years she has learned a cue and jumps up quickly to visit anyone sitting on the sofa. She learned by herself that all guests on the sofa were to be trusted friends. I think she felt more comfortable with them being at her level, rather than towering over her.

Dogs can be afraid of numerous things, including loud noises and thunderstorms. Invariably the owner rewards (by comforting) the dog when it shows signs of fearfulness. I had a terrible problem with my favorite dog in the Utility

Shih Tzu will look to their owner for comfort and support during times of fear and insecurity.

obedience class. Not only was he intimidated in the class but he was afraid of noise and afraid of displeasing me. Frequently he would knock down the bar jump, which clattered dreadfully. I gave him credit because he continued to try to clear it, although he was terribly scared. I

For the safety of your Shih Tzu, be sure that your yard is securely fenced.

finally learned to "reward" him every time he knocked down the jump. I would jump up and down, clap my hands and tell him how great he was. My psychology worked, he relaxed and eventually cleared the jump with ease. When your dog is frightened, direct his attention to something else and act happy. Don't dwell on his fright.

A Shih Tzu who feels secure will wander into many different areas when permitted to roam, even your flower bed!

PROBLEMS

Barking

This is a habit that shouldn't be encouraged. Over the years I've had new puppy owners call to say that their dog hasn't learned to bark. I assure them they are indeed fortunate but not to worry. Some owners desire their dog to bark so as to be a watchdog. In my experience, most dogs will bark when a stranger comes to the door.

The new puppy frequently barks or whines in the crate in his strange environment and the owner reinforces the puppy's bad behavior by going to him during the night. This is a no-no. I tell my new owners to smack the top of the crate and say "quiet" in a loud, firm voice. The puppies don't like to hear the loud noise of the crate being banged. If the barking is sleep-interrupting, then the owner should take crate and pup to the bedroom for a few days until the puppy becomes adjusted to his new environment. Otherwise ignore the barking during the night.

Barking can be an inherited problem or a bad habit learned through the environment. It takes dedication to stop the barking. Attention should be paid to the cause of the barking. Does the dog seek attention, does he need to go out, is it feeding time, is it occurring when he is left alone, is it a protective bark, etc.? Presently I have a ten-week-old puppy that is a real loud mouth, which I am

A puppy can inherit its barkiness from its parents, or it may be learned through the environment.

Barking is a habit that shouldn't be encouraged. Do not be worried if your dog seems not to bark, think of it as a blessing!

A barking dog can become a nuisance to your neighbors. Be courteous and try to keep your Shih Tzu from barking while outdoors.

sure is an inherited tendency. Both her mother and especially her grandmother are overzealous barkers but fortunately have mellowed with the years. My young puppy is corrected with a firm "no" and gentle shaking and she is responding. When barking presents a problem for you, try to stop it as soon as it begins.

There are electronic collars available that are supposed to curb barking. Personally I have not had experience with them. There are some disadvantages to to the collar. If the dog is barking out of excitement, punishment is not the appropriate treatment. Presumably there is the chance the collar could be activated by other stimuli and thereby punish the dog when it is not barking. Should you decide to use one, then you should seek help from a person with experience with that type of collar. In my opinion I feel the root of the problem needs to be investigated and corrected.

In extreme circumstances (usually when there is a problem with the neighbors), some people have resorted to having their dogs debarked. I caution you that the dog continues to bark but usually only a squeaking sound is heard. Frequently the vocal cords grow back. Probably the biggest concern is that the dog can be left with scar tissue which can narrow the opening to the trachea. A dog was sent to me for breeding that overheated on the airplane. When I notified the owner, she said the dog had been debarked and was left with scar tissue.

Biting

All puppies bite and try to chew on your fingers, toes, arms, etc. This is the time to teach them to be gentle and not bite hard. Put your fingers in your puppy's mouth and if he bites too hard then say "easy" and let him know he's hurting you. I squeal and act like I have been seriously hurt. If the puppy plays too rough and doesn't respond to your corrections, then he needs "Time Out" in his crate. You should be particularly careful with young children and puppies who still have their deciduous (baby) teeth. Those teeth are like needles and can leave little scars on youngsters. My adult daughter still has a small scar on her face from when she teased an eight-week-old puppy as an eight year old.

Biting and chewing is natural for puppies and should be encouraged. Do not leave out shoes or other valuables that your puppy may attempt to chew.

Brushing your Shih Tzu three or four times a week will help to avoid the coat matting.

Biting in the more mature dog is something that should be prevented at all costs. Should it occur I would quickly let him know in no uncertain terms that biting will not be tolerated. When biting is directed toward another dog (dog fight), don't get in the middle of it. On more than one occasion I have had to separate a couple of my dogs and usually was in the middle of that one last lunge by the offender. Some authorities recommend breaking up a fight by elevating the hind legs. This

A Shih Tzu puppy is very impressionable and should be trained early.

would only be possible if there was a person for each dog. Obviously it would be hard to fight with the hind legs off the ground. A dog bite is serious and should be given attention. Wash the bite with soap and water and contact your doctor. It is important to know the status of the offender's rabies vaccination.

I have several dogs that are sensitive to having mats combed out of their coats and eventually they have had enough. They give fair warning by turning and acting like they would like to nip my offending fingers. However, one verbal warning from me says, "I'm sorry, don't you dare think about biting me and please let me carefully comb just a little bit more." I have owned a minimum of 30 dogs and raised many more puppies and have yet to have one of my dogs bite me except during that last lunge in the two or three dog fights I felt compelled to break up. My dogs wouldn't dare bite me. They know who is boss.

This is not always the case for other owners. I do not wish to frighten you but when biting occurs you should seek professional help at once. On the other hand you must not let your dog intimidate you and be so afraid of a bite that you can't discipline him. Professional help through your veterinarian, dog trainer and/or behaviorist can give you guidance.

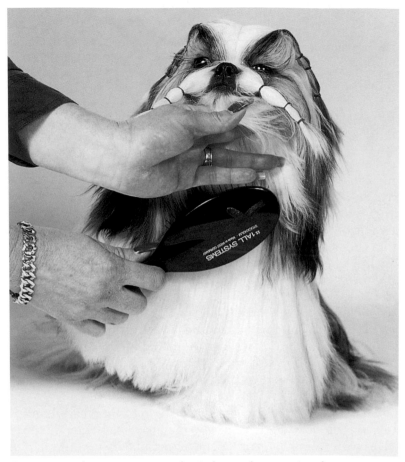

Be sure to gently groom your pet so that it does not become agitated.

Submissive Urination

This is not a housebreaking problem. It can occur in all breeds and may be more prevalent in some breeds. Usually it occurs in puppies but occasionally it occurs in older dogs and may be in response to physical praise. Try verbal praise or ignoring your dog until after he has had a chance to relieve himself. Scolding will only make the problem worse. Many dogs outgrow this problem.

Coprophagia

Also know as stool eating, sometimes occurs without a cause. It may begin with boredom and then becomes a habit that is hard to break. Your best remedy is to keep the puppy on a leash and keep the yard picked up. Then he won't have an opportunity to get in trouble. I do not like to clean up accidents or "poop scoop" the yard in front of puppies. I'm suspicious that some puppies try to help and will clean up the stool before I have a chance. Your veterinarian can dispense a medication that is put on the dog's food that makes the stool taste bitter. Of course this will do little good if your dog cleans up after other dogs.

Mischief and Misbehavior

All puppies and even some adult dogs will get into mischief at some time in their lives. You should start by "puppy proofing" your house. Even so it is impossible to have a sterile environment. For instance, if you would be down to four walls and a floor your dog could still chew a hole in the wall. What do you do? Remember puppies should never be left unsupervised so let us go on to the trusted adult dog that has misbehaved. His behavior may be an attention getter. Dogs, and even children, are known to do mischief even though they know they will be punished. Your puppy/dog will benefit from more attention and new direction. He may benefit from a training class or by reinforcing the obedience he has already learned. How about a daily walk? That could be a good outlet for your dog, time together and exercise for both of you.

By keeping your Shih Tzu on a fixed schedule you will avoid housetraining accidents.

All puppies and dogs will benefit from more attention and more interaction with their owners. Shih Tzu that are bored are not happy pets.

Separation Anxiety

This occurs when dogs feel distress or apprehension when separated from their owners. One of the mistakes owners make is to set their dogs up for their departure. Some authorities recommend paying little attention to the pet for at least ten minutes before leaving and for the first ten minutes after you arrive home. The dog isn't cued to the fact you are leaving and if you keep it lowkey they learn to accept it as a normal everyday occurrence. Those dogs that are used to being crated usually accept your departure. Dogs that are anxious may have a serious problem and wreak havoc on the house within a few minutes after your departure. You can try to acclimate your dog to the separation by leaving for just a few minutes at a time, returning and rewarding him with a treat. Don't get too carried away. Plan on this process taking a long time. A behaviorist can set down a schedule for you. Those dogs that are insecure, such as ones obtained from a humane shelter or those that have changed homes, present more of a problem.

Punishment

A puppy should learn that correction is sometimes necessary and should not question your authority. An older

A crate may be the only way you will be able to keep your Shih Tzu out of trouble during the periods that you cannot supervise him.

Encouraging good habits is more effective than punishment.

dog that has never received correction may retaliate. In my opinion there will be a time for physical punishment but this does not mean hitting the dog. Do not use newspapers, fly swatters, etc. One type of correction, that is used by the mother dog when she corrects her puppies, is to take the puppy by the scruff and shake him *gently*. For the older, larger dog you can grab the scruff, one hand on each side of his neck, and lift his legs off the ground. This is effective since dogs feel intimidated when their feet are off the ground. Timing is of the utmost importance when punishment is necessary. Depending on the degree of fault, you might want to reinforce punishment by ignoring your dog for 15 to 20 minutes. Whatever you do, do not overdo corrections or they will lose value.

My most important advice to you is to be aware of your dog's actions. Even so, remember dogs are dogs and will behave as such even though we might like them to be perfect little people. You and your dog will become neurotic if you worry about every little indiscretion. When there is reason for concern—don't waste time. Seek guidance. Dogs are meant to be loved and enjoyed.

References:
Manual of Canine Behavior, Valerie O'Farrell, British Small Animal Veterinary Association.

Good Owners, Great Dogs, Brian Kilcommons, Warner Books.

TRAVELING with Your Dog

When planning a family vacation one of the first things to consider is what to do with the dog. Shih Tzu on a whole do not kennel well, they are so people oriented that they tend to pine and rarely do well in a large kennel. It sure is not like home, no chair, bed or lap to crawl into. I started with my first litter of pups, worrying what the new owners would do with my babies when they went away. I guess my puppy owners are lucky— I offered to babysit! If there is no aunt or uncle, no sister or brother, what better place then to go to camp at Grandma's Of course everyone is not so lucky, so be sure to consider this when you decide to own a Shih Tzu. Please find them a loving place to stay when you are away.

The earlier you start traveling with your new puppy or dog, the better. He needs to become accustomed to traveling. However, some dogs are nervous riders and become carsick easily. It is helpful if he starts with an empty stomach. Do not despair, as it will go

Family vacation can be very enjoyable when you bring your Shih Tzu along.

118

better if you continue taking him with you on short fun rides. How would you feel if every time you rode in the car you stopped at the doctor's for an injection? You would soon dread that nasty car. Older dogs that tend to get carsick may have more of a problem adjusting to traveling. Those dogs that are having a serious problem may benefit from

A Show Shih Tzu spends a great deal of time traveling. This they get used to and enjoy.

some medication prescribed by the veterinarian.

Do give your dog a chance to relieve himself before getting into the car. It is a good idea to be prepared for a clean up with a leash, paper towels, bag and terry cloth towel.

The safest place for your dog is in a fiberglass crate, although

You should never ride in your car with your dog on your lap, no matter what breed. This is hazardous to your driving and dangerous for your pet.

If you must take a long journey, be sure to stop several times and allow your Shih Tzu to relieve itself.

close confinement can promote carsickness in some dogs. If your dog is nervous you can try letting him ride on the seat next to you or in someone's lap.

An alternative to the crate would be to use a car harness made for dogs and/or a safety strap attached to the harness or collar. Whatever you do, do not let your dog ride in the back of a pickup truck unless he is securely tied on a very short lead. I've seen trucks stop quickly and, even though the dog was tied, it fell out and was dragged.

I do occasionally let my dogs ride loose with me because I really enjoy their companionship, but in all honesty they are safer in their crates. I have a friend whose van rolled in an accident but his dogs, in their fiberglass crates, were not injured nor did they escape. Another advantage of the crate is that it is a safe place to leave him if you need to run into the store. Otherwise you wouldn't be able to leave the windows down. Keep in mind that while many dogs are overly protective in their crates, this may not be enough to deter dognappers. In some states it is against the law to leave a dog in the car unattended.

Never leave a dog loose in the car wearing a collar and leash. I have known more than one dog that has killed himself by hanging.

Do not let him put his head out an open window. Foreign debris can be blown into his eyes. When leaving your dog unattended in a car, consider the temperature. It can take less than five minutes to reach temperatures over 100 degrees.

TRIPS

Perhaps you are taking a trip. Give consideration to what is best for your dog—traveling with you or boarding. When traveling by car, van or motor home, you need to think ahead about locking your vehicle. In all probability you have many valuables in the car and do not wish to leave it unlocked. Perhaps most valuable and not replaceable is your dog. Give thought to securing your vehicle and providing adequate ventilation for him. Another consideration for you when traveling with your dog is medical problems that may arise and little inconveniences, such as exposure to external parasites. Some areas of the country are quite flea infested. You may want to carry flea spray with

A crate is a necessary piece of equipment if you plan to travel with your dog.

An exercise pen is a great way to allow your pet plenty of activity while you stop on the road.

you. This is even a good idea when staying in motels. Quite possibly you are not the only occupant of the room.

Unbelievably many motels and even hotels do allow canine guests, even some very first-class ones. Gaines Pet Foods Corporation publishes *Touring With Towser*, a directory of domestic hotels and motels that accommodate guests with dogs. Their address is Gaines TWT, PO Box 5700, Kankakee, IL, 60902. I would recommend you call ahead to any motel that you may be considering and see if they accept pets. Sometimes it is necessary to pay a deposit against room damage. Of course you are more likely to gain accommodations for a small dog than a large dog. Also the management feels reassured when you mention that your dog will be crated. Since my dogs tend to bark when I leave the room, I leave the TV on nearly full blast to deaden the noises outside that tend to encourage my dogs to bark. If you do travel with your dog, take along plenty of baggies so that you can clean up after him. When we all do our share in cleaning up, we make it possible for motels to continue accepting our pets. As a matter of fact, you should practice cleaning up everywhere you take your dog.

Depending on where your are traveling, you may need an up-to-date health certificate issued by your veterinarian. It is good policy to take along your dog's medical information, which would include the name, address and phone number of your veterinarian, vaccination record, rabies certificate, and any medication he is taking.

AIR TRAVEL

When traveling by air, you need to contact the airlines to check their policy. Usually you have to make arrangements up to a couple of weeks in advance for traveling with your dog. The airlines require your dog to travel in an airline approved fiberglass crate. Usually these can be purchased through the airlines but they are also readily available in most pet-supply stores. If your dog is not accustomed to a crate, then it is a good idea to get him acclimated to it before your trip. The day of the actual trip you should withhold water about one hour ahead of departure and no food for about 12 hours. The airlines generally have temperature restrictions, which do not allow pets to travel if it is either too cold or too hot. Frequently these restrictions are based on the temperatures at the departure and arrival airports.

It's best to inquire about a health certificate. These usually need to be issued within ten days of departure. You should arrange for non-stop, direct flights and if a commuter plane should be involved, check to see if it will carry dogs. Some don't. The Humane Society of the United States has put together a tip sheet for airline traveling. You can receive a copy by sending a self-addressed stamped envelope to:

The Humane Society of the United States
Tip Sheet
2100 L Street NW
Washington, DC 20037.

Regulations differ for traveling outside of the country and are sometimes changed without notice. Well in advance you need to write or call the appropriate consulate or agricultural department for instructions. Some countries have lengthy quarantines (six months), and countries differ in their rabies vaccination requirements. For instance, it may have to be given at least 30 days ahead of your departure.

Do make sure your dog is wearing proper identification. You never know when you might be in an accident and separated from your dog. Or your dog could be frightened and somehow manage to escape and

Being very accommodating dogs, Shih Tzu usually fare well on vacation.

run away. When I travel, my dogs wear collars with engraved nameplates with my name, phone number and city.

Another suggestion would be to carry in-case-of-emergency instructions. These would include the address and phone number of a relative or friend, your

Reputable boarding kennels will allow your Shih Tzu plenty of exercise as well as provide a safe environment while you are away.

veterinarian's name, address and phone number, and your dog's medical information.

BOARDING KENNELS

Perhaps you have decided that you need to board your dog. Your veterinarian can recommend a good boarding facility or possibly a pet sitter that will come to your house. It is customary for the boarding kennel to ask for proof of vaccination for the DHLPP, rabies and bordetella vaccine. The bordetella should have been given within six months of boarding. This is for your protection. If they do not ask for this proof I would not board at their kennel. Ask about flea control. Those dogs that suffer flea-bite allergy can get in trouble at a boarding kennel. Unfortunately boarding kennels are limited on how much they are able to do.

For more information on pet sitting, contact NAPPS:
National Association of Professional Pet Sitters
1200 G Street, NW
Suite 760
Washington, DC 20005.

Our clinic has technicians that pet sit and technicians that board clinic patients in their homes. This may be an alternative for you. Ask your veterinarian if they have an employee that can help you. There is a definite advantage of having a technician care for your dog, especially if your dog is on medication or is a senior citizen.

You can write for a copy of *Traveling With Your Pet* from ASPCA, Education Department, 441 E. 92nd Street, New York, NY 10128.

IDENTIFICATION and Finding the Lost Dog

There are several ways of identifying your dog. The old standby is a collar with dog license, rabies, and ID tags. Unfortunately collars have a way of being separated from the dog and tags fall off. I am not suggesting you shouldn't use a collar and tags. If they stay intact and on the dog, they are the quickest way of identification. For several years owners have been tattooing their dogs. Some tattoos use a number with a registry. Here lies the problem because there are several registries to check. If you wish to tattoo, use your social security number. The humane shelters have the means to trace it. It is usually done on the inside of the rear thigh. The area is first shaved and numbed. There is no pain, although a few dogs do not like the buzzing sound. Occasionally tattooing is not legible and needs to be redone.

The newest method of identification is microchipping. The microchip is a computer chip that is no larger than a grain of rice. The veterinarian implants it by injection between the shoulder blades. The dog feels no discomfort. If your dog is lost

No matter what the season, your Shih Tzu will fill your life with lots of love and happiness.

and picked up by the humane society, they can trace you by scanning the microchip, which has its own code. Microchip scanners are friendly to other brands of microchips and their registries. The microchip comes with a dog tag saying the dog is microchipped. It is the safest way of identifying your dog.

FINDING THE LOST DOG

I am sure you will agree with me that there would be little worse than losing your dog. Responsible pet owners rarely lose their dogs. They do not

Tying up your Shih Tzu's topknot helps your dog's vision as well as gives it that special Shih Tzu look.

let their dogs run free because they don't want harm to come to them. Not only that but in most, if not all, states there is a leash law. Beware of fenced-in yards. They can be a hazard. Dogs find ways

Shih Tzu definitely know when their owners have left them. They sit and pine for long hours just waiting for their masters to return

Hiding among a group of leaves can't conceal this cute Shih Tzu.

to escape either over or under the fence. Another fast exit is through the gate that perhaps the neighbor's child left unlocked.

Below is a list that hopefully will be of help to you if you need it. Remember don't give up, keep looking. Your dog is worth your efforts.

Should your Shih Tzu become lost, contact breeders and rescue groups for your breed so they can be on the lookout for your pet.

1 Contact your neighbors and put flyers with a photo on it in their mailboxes. Information you should include would be the dog's name, breed, sex, color, age, source of identification, when your dog was last seen and where, and your name and phone numbers. It may be helpful to say the dog needs medical care. Offer a *reward*.

2. Check all local shelters daily. It is also possible for your dog to be picked up away from home and end up in an out-of-the-way shelter. Check these too. Go in person. It is not good enough to call. Most shelters are limited on the time they can hold dogs then they are put up for adoption or euthanized. There is the possibility that your dog will not make it to the shelter for several days. Your dog could have been wandering or someone may have tried to keep him.

3. Notify all local veterinarians. Call and send flyers.

4. Call your breeder. Frequently breeders are contacted when one of their breed is found.

5. Contact the rescue group for your breed.

6. Contact local schools—children may have seen your dog.

7. Post flyers at the schools, groceries, gas stations, convenience stores, veterinary clinics, groomers and any other place that will allow them.

8. Advertise in the newspaper.

9. Advertise on the radio.

DENTAL CARE for Your Dog's Life

So you've got a new puppy! You also have a new set of puppy teeth in your household. Anyone who has ever raised a puppy is abundantly aware of these new teeth. Your puppy will chew anything it can reach, chase your shoelaces, and play "tear the rag" with any piece of clothing it can find. When puppies are newly born, they have no teeth. At about four weeks of age, puppies of most breeds begin to develop their deciduous or baby teeth. They begin eating semi-solid food, fighting and biting with their litter mates, and learning discipline from their mother. As their new teeth come in, they inflict more pain on their mother's breasts, so her feeding sessions become less frequent and shorter. By six or eight weeks, the mother will start growling to warn her pups when they are fighting too roughly or hurting her as they nurse too much with their new teeth.

Puppies need to chew. It is a necessary part of their physical and mental development. They develop muscles and necessary life skills as they drag objects around, fight over possession, and vocalize alerts and warnings. Puppies chew on things to explore their world. They are using their sense of taste to determine what is food and what is not. How else can they tell an electrical cord from a lizard? At about four months of age, most puppies begin shedding their baby teeth. Often these teeth need some help to come out and make

All dogs need safe chew toys to keep their teeth and jaws occupied.

Toys and bones can be used for a reward during training sessions.

way for the permanent teeth. The incisors (front teeth) will be replaced first. Then, the adult canine or fang teeth erupt. When the baby tooth is not shed before the permanent tooth comes in, veterinarians call it a retained deciduous tooth. This condition will often cause gum infections by trapping hair and debris between the permanent tooth and the retained baby tooth. Nylafloss® is an excellent device for puppies to use. They can toss it, drag it, and chew on the many surfaces it presents. The baby teeth can catch in the nylon material, aiding in their removal. Puppies that have adequate chew toys will have less destructive behavior, develop more physically, and have less chance of retained deciduous teeth.

During the first year, your dog should be seen by your veterinarian at regular intervals. Your veterinarian will let you know when to bring in your puppy for vaccinations and parasite examinations. At each visit, your veterinarian should inspect the lips, teeth, and mouth as part of a complete physical examination. You should take some part in the maintenance of your dog's oral health. You should examine your dog's mouth weekly throughout his first year to make sure there are no sores, foreign objects, tooth problems, etc. If your dog drools excessively, shakes its head, or has bad breath, consult your veterinarian. By the time your dog is six months old, the permanent teeth are all in and plaque can start to accumulate on the

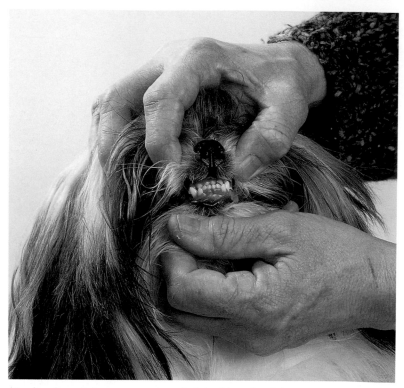

Good oral care is important to your dog's health and well-being.

tooth surfaces. This is when your dog needs to develop good dental-care habits to prevent calculus build-up on its teeth. Brushing is best. That is a fact that cannot be denied. However, some dogs do not like their teeth brushed regularly, or you may not be able to accomplish the task. In that case, you should consider a product that will help prevent plaque and calculus build-up.

The Dental Chews® and Galileo Bone® are other excellent choices for the first three years of a dog's life. Their shapes make them interesting for the dog. As the dog chews on them, the solid polyurethane massages the gums which improves the blood circulation to the periodontal tissues. Projections on the chew devices increase the surface and are in contact with the tooth for more efficient cleaning. The unique shape and consistency prevent your dog from exerting excessive force on his own teeth or from breaking off pieces of the bone. If your dog is an aggressive chewer or weighs more than 55 pounds (25 kg), you should consider giving him a Nylabone®, the most durable chew product on the market.

By the time dogs are four years old, 75% of them have periodontal disease. It is the most common infection in dogs. Yearly examinations by your veterinarian are essential to maintaining your dog's good health. If your veterinarian detects periodontal disease, he or she may recommend a prophylactic cleaning. To do a thorough cleaning, it will be necessary to put your dog under anesthesia. With modern gas anesthetics and monitoring equipment, the procedure is pretty safe. Your veterinarian will scale the teeth with an ultrasound scaler or hand instrument. This removes the calculus from the teeth. If there are calculus deposits below the gum line, the veterinarian will plane the roots to make them smooth. After all of the calculus has been removed, the teeth are polished with pumice in a polishing cup. If any medical or surgical treatment is needed, it is done at this time. The final step would be fluoride treatment and your follow-up treatment at home. If the periodontal disease is advanced, the veterinarian may prescribe a mediated mouth rinse or antibiotics for use at home. Make sure your dog has safe, clean and attractive chew toys and treats. Chooz® treats are another way of using a consumable treat to help keep your dog's teeth clean.

Rawhide is the most popular of all materials for a dog to chew. This has never been good news to dog owners, because rawhide is inherently very dangerous for dogs. Thousands of dogs have died

Good nutrition and care will be evident in your dog's healthy appearance and enthusiastic attitude.

from rawhide, having swallowed the hide after it has become soft and mushy, only to cause stomach and intestinal blockage. A new rawhide product on the market has finally solved the problem of rawhide: molded Roar-Hide® from Nylabone. These are composed of processed, cut up, and melted American rawhide injected into your dog's favorite shape: a dog bone. These dog-safe devices smell and taste like rawhide but don't break up. The ridges on the bones help to fight tartar build-up on the teeth and they last ten times longer than the usual rawhide chews.

As your dog ages, professional examination and cleaning should become more frequent. The mouth should be inspected at least once a year. Your veterinarian may recommend visits every six months. In the geriatric patient, organs such as the heart, liver, and kidneys do not function as well as when they were young. Your veterinarian will probably want to test these organs' functions prior to using general anesthesia for dental cleaning. If your dog is a good chewer and you work closely with your veterinarian, your dog can keep all of its teeth all

Check your Shih Tzu's teeth and mouth as part of his regular grooming routine.

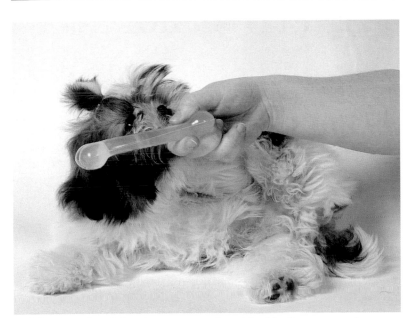

Nylabone® products help to keep your puppy's teeth healthy. Be sure to supply your pet with plenty of these pacifiers.

of its life. However, as your dog ages, his sense of smell, sight, and taste will diminish. He may not have the desire to chase, trap or chew his toys. He will also not have the energy to chew for long periods, as arthritis and periodontal disease make chewing painful. This will leave you with more responsibility for keeping his teeth clean and healthy. The dog that would not let you brush his teeth at one year of age, may let you brush his teeth now that he is ten years old.

If you train your dog with good chewing habits as a puppy, he will have healthier teeth throughout his life.

HEALTH CARE for Your Shih Tzu

Veterinary medicine has become far more sophisticated than what was available to our ancestors. This can be attributed to the increase in household pets and consequently the demand for better care for them. Also human medicine has become far more complex. Today diagnostic testing in veterinary medicine parallels human diagnostics. Because of better technology we can expect our pets to live healthier lives thereby increasing their life spans.

THE FIRST CHECK UP

You will want to take your new puppy/dog in for its first check up within 48 to 72 hours after acquiring it. Many breeders strongly recommend this check up and so do the humane shelters. A puppy/dog can appear healthy but it may have a serious problem that is not apparent to the layman. Most pets have some type of a minor flaw that may never cause a real problem.

Unfortunately if he/she should have a serious problem, you will want to consider the consequences of keeping the pet and the attachments that will be formed, which may be broken prematurely. Keep in mind there are many healthy dogs looking for good homes.

This first check up is a good time to establish yourself with the veterinarian and learn the office policy regarding their hours and how they handle emergencies. Usually the breeder or another conscientious pet owner is a good reference for locating a capable veterinarian. You should be aware that not all veterinarians give the same quality of service. Please do not make your selection on the least expensive clinic, as they may be short changing your pet. There is the possibility that eventually it will cost you more due to improper diagnosis, treatment, etc. If you are selecting a new veterinarian, feel free to ask for a tour of the clinic. You should inquire about making an appointment for a tour since all clinics are working clinics, and therefore may not be available all day for sightseers. You may worry less if you see where your pet will be spending the day if he ever needs to be hospitalized.

Your Shih Tzu's health is important from the very first day you bring him home. As a pet, it will rely on you to care for it and provide the very best health care that you can.

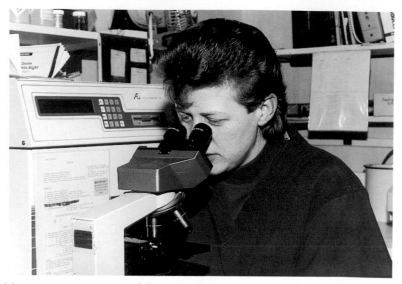

Most veterinary practices are fully equipped. Ideally, you can have tests performed and results given back to you all in the same day.

THE PHYSICAL EXAM

Your veterinarian will check your pet's overall condition, which includes listening to the heart; checking the respiration; feeling the abdomen, muscles and joints; checking the mouth, which includes the gum color and signs of gum disease along with plaque buildup; checking the ears for signs of an infection or ear mites; examining the eyes; and, last but not least, checking the condition of the skin and coat.

He should ask you questions regarding your pet's eating and elimination habits and invite you to relay your questions. It is a good idea to prepare a list so as not to forget anything. He should discuss the proper diet and the quantity to be fed. If this should differ from your breeder's recommendation, then you should convey to him the breeder's choice and see if he approves. If he recommends changing the diet, then this should be done over a few days so as not to cause a gastrointestinal upset. It is customary to take in a fresh stool sample (just a small amount) for a test for intestinal parasites. It must be fresh, preferably within 12 hours, since the eggs hatch quickly and after hatching will not be observed under the microscope. If your pet isn't obliging then, usually the technician can take one in the clinic.

IMMUNIZATIONS

It is important that you take your puppy/dog's vaccination record with you on your first visit. In case of a puppy, presumably the breeder has seen to the vaccinations up to the time you acquired custody. Veterinarians differ in their vaccination protocol. It is not unusual for your puppy to have received vaccinations for distemper, hepatitis, leptospirosis, parvovirus and parainfluenza every two to three weeks from the age of five or six weeks. Usually this is a combined injection and is typically called the DHLPP. The DHLPP is given through at least 12 to 14 weeks of age, and it is customary to continue with another parvovirus vaccine at 16 to 18 weeks. You may wonder why so many immunizations are necessary. No one knows for sure when the puppy's maternal antibodies are gone, although it is customarily accepted that distemper antibodies are gone by 12 weeks. Usually parvovirus antibodies are gone by 16 to 18 weeks of age. However, it is possible for the maternal antibodies to be gone at a much earlier age or even a later age. Therefore immunizations are started at an early age. The vaccine will not give immunity as long as there are maternal antibodies.

A listless or otherwise disinterested pet may be cause to see your veterinarian.

Your Shih Tzu will be able to live a long healthy life with you provided it receives the very best care.

The rabies vaccination is given at three or six months of age depending on your local laws. A vaccine for bordetella (kennel cough) is advisable and can be given anytime from the age of five weeks. The coronavirus is not commonly given unless there is a problem locally. The Lyme vaccine is necessary in endemic areas. Lyme disease has been reported in 47 states.

Distemper

This is virtually an incurable disease. If the dog recovers, he is subject to severe nervous disorders. The virus attacks every tissue in the body and resembles a bad cold with a fever. It can cause a runny nose and eyes and cause gastrointestinal disorders, including a poor appetite, vomiting and diarrhea. The virus is carried by raccoons, foxes, wolves, mink and other dogs. Unvaccinated youngsters and senior citizens are very susceptible. This is still a common disease.

Hepatitis

This is a virus that is most serious in very young dogs. It is spread by contact with an infected animal or its stool or urine. The virus affects the liver and kidneys and is characterized by high fever, depression and lack of appetite. Recovered animals may be afflicted with chronic illnesses.

Leptospirosis

This is a bacterial disease transmitted by contact with the urine of an infected dog, rat or other wildlife. It produces severe symptoms of fever, depression, jaundice and internal bleeding and was fatal before the vaccine was developed. Recovered dogs can be carriers, and the disease can be transmitted from dogs to humans.

Parvovirus

This was first noted in the late 1970s and is still a fatal disease. However, with proper vaccinations, early diagnosis and prompt treatment, it is a manageable disease. It attacks the bone marrow and intestinal tract. The symptoms include depression, loss of appetite, vomiting, diarrhea and collapse. Immediate medical attention is of the essence.

Rabies

This is shed in the saliva and is carried by raccoons, skunks, foxes, other dogs and cats. It attacks nerve tissue, resulting in paralysis and death. Rabies can be transmitted to people and is virtually always fatal. This disease is reappearing in the suburbs.

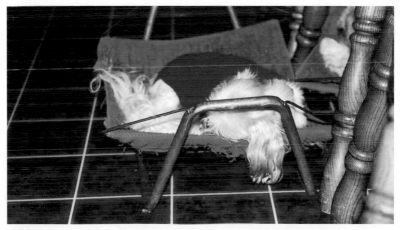

Telltale signs that your Shih Tzu is not feeling well would be any sudden changes in its personality, eating habits or activity level.

Bordetella (Kennel Cough)

The symptoms are coughing, sneezing, hacking and retching accompanied by nasal discharge usually lasting from a few days to several weeks. There are several disease-producing organisms responsible for this disease. The present vaccines are helpful but do not protect for all the strains. It usually is not life threatening but in some instances it can progress to a serious bronchopneumonia. The disease is highly contagious. The vaccination should be given routinely for dogs that come in contact with other dogs, such as through boarding, training class or visits to the groomer.

Coronavirus

This is usually self limiting and not life threatening. It was first noted in the late '70s about a year before parvovirus. The virus produces a yellow/brown stool and there may be depression, vomiting and diarrhea.

Lyme Disease

This was first diagnosed in the United States in 1976 in Lyme, CT in people who lived in close proximity to the deer tick. Symptoms may include acute lameness, fever, swelling of joints and loss of appetite. Your veterinarian can advise you if you live in an endemic area.

Puppies are susceptible to illnesses because they have not yet built up an immune system.

After your puppy has completed his puppy vaccinations, you will continue to booster the DHLPP once a year. It is customary to booster the rabies one year after the first vaccine and then, depending on where you live, it should be boostered every year or every three years. This depends on your local laws. The Lyme and corona vaccines are boostered annually and it is recommended that the bordetella be boostered every six to eight months.

Fleas and ticks can be picked up from the outdoors. Be sure to check your Shih Tzu thoroughly each time it returns indoors.

ANNUAL VISIT

I would like to impress the importance of the annual check up, which would include the booster vaccinations, check for

During its first year, a Shih Tzu puppy will have to visit a veterinarian for three sets of shots, the last of which should be administered at 14-16 weeks.

intestinal parasites and test for heartworm. Today in our very busy world it is rush, rush and see "how much you can get for how little." Unbelievably, some non-veterinary businesses have entered into the vaccination business. More harm than good can come to your dog through improper vaccinations, possibly from inferior vaccines and/or the wrong schedule. More than likely you truly care about your companion dog and over the years you have devoted much time and expense to his well being. Perhaps you are unaware that a vaccination is not just a vaccination. There is more involved. Please, please follow through with regular physical examinations. It is so important for your veterinarian to know your dog and this is especially true during middle age through the geriatric years. More than likely your older dog will require more than one physical a year. The annual physical is good preventive medicine. Through early diagnosis and subsequent treatment your dog can maintain a longer and better quality of life.

INTESTINAL PARASITES

Hookworms

These are an almost microscopic intestinal worms that can cause anemia and therefore serious problems, including death, in young puppies. Hookworms can be transmitted to humans through penetration of the skin. Puppies may be born with them.

Roundworms

These are spaghetti-like worms that can cause a potbellied appearance and dull coat along with more severe symptoms, such as vomiting, diarrhea and coughing. Puppies acquire these while in the mother's uterus and through lactation. Both hookworms and roundworms may be acquired through ingestion.

Whipworms

These have a three-month life cycle and are not acquired through the dam. They cause intermittent diarrhea usually with mucus. Whipworms are possibly the most difficult worm to eradicate. Their eggs are very resistant to most environmental factors and can last for years until the proper conditions enable them to mature. Whipworms are seldom seen in the stool.

Your Shih Tzu's overall health is most important; that is why annual visits to the veterinarian are important.

Whipworms are not acquired through the dam. They are the hardest worm to irradiate.

Intestinal parasites are more prevalent in some areas than others. Climate, soil and contamination are big factors contributing to the incidence of intestinal parasites. Eggs are passed in the stool, lay on the ground and then become infective in a certain number of days. Each of the above worms has a different life cycle. Your best chance of becoming and remaining worm-free is to always pooper-scoop your yard. A fenced-in yard keeps stray dogs out, which is certainly helpful.

I would recommend having a fecal examination on your dog twice a year or more often if there is a problem. If your dog has a positive fecal sample, then he will be given the appropriate medication and you will be asked to bring back another stool sample in a certain period of time (depending on the type of worm) and then be rewormed. This process goes on until he has at least two negative samples. The different types of worms require different medications. You will be wasting your money and doing your dog an injustice by buying over-the-counter medication without first consulting your veterinarian.

OTHER INTERNAL PARASITES

Coccidiosis and Giardiasis
These protozoal infections usually affect puppies, especially in places where large numbers of puppies are brought together. Older dogs may harbor these infections but do not show signs unless they are stressed. Symptoms include diarrhea, weight loss and lack of appetite. These infections are not always apparent in the fecal examination.

Tapeworms
Seldom apparent on fecal floatation, they are diagnosed frequently as rice-like segments around the dog's anus and the base of the tail. Tapeworms are long, flat and ribbon like, sometimes several feet in length, and made up of many segments about five-eighths of an inch long. The two most common types of tapeworms found in the dog are.

(1) First the larval form of the flea tapeworm parasite must mature in an intermediate host, the flea, before it can become infective. Your dog acquires this by ingesting the flea through licking and chewing.

(2) Rabbits, rodents and certain large game animals serve as intermediate hosts for other species of tapeworms. If your dog should eat one of these infected hosts, then he can acquire tapeworms.

HEARTWORM DISEASE
This is a worm that resides in the heart and adjacent blood vessels of the lung that produces microfilaria, which circulate in the bloodstream. It is possible for a dog to be infected with any number of worms from one

Adult whipworms. Whipworms cause intermittent diarrhea usually with mucus.

Heartworm, a disease transmitted through a mosquito, is life threatening. It is expensive to treat but can be easily avoided through monthly preventatives.

to a hundred that can be 6 to 14 inches long. It is a life-threatening disease, expensive to treat and easily prevented. Depending on where you live, your veterinarian may recommend a preventive year-round and either an annual or semiannual blood test. The most common preventive is given once a month.

EXTERNAL PARASITES

Fleas

These pests are not only the dog's worst enemy but also enemy to the owner's pocketbook. Preventing is less expensive than treating, but regardless I think we'd prefer to spend our money elsewhere. I would guess that the majority of our dogs are allergic to the bite of a flea, and in many cases it only takes one flea bite. The protein in the flea's saliva is the culprit. Allergic dogs have a reaction, which usually results in a "hot spot." More than likely such a reaction will involve a trip to the veterinarian for treatment. Yes, prevention is less expensive. Fortunately today there are several good products available.

If there is a flea infestation, no one product is going to correct the problem. Not only will the dog require treatment so will the environment. In general flea collars are not very effective although there is now available an "egg" collar that will kill the eggs on the dog. Dips are the most economical but they are messy. There are some effective shampoos and treatments available through pet shops and veterinarians. An oral tablet arrived on the American market in 1995 and was popular in Europe the previous year. It sterilizes the female flea but will not kill adult fleas. Therefore the tablet, which is given monthly, will decrease the flea population but is not a "cure-all." Those dogs that suffer from flea-bite allergy will still be subjected to the bite of the flea. Another popular parasiticide is permethrin, which is applied to the back of the dog in one or two places depending on the dog's weight. This product works as a repellent causing the flea to get "hot feet" and jump off. Do not confuse this product with some of the organophosphates that are also applied to the dog's back.

Some products are not usable on young puppies. Treating fleas should be done under your veterinarian's guidance. Frequently it is necessary to combine products and the layman does not have the knowledge regarding possible toxicities. It is hard to believe but

Ch. Lainee Lucy is well cared for by owner Lynne Bennett.

there are a few dogs that do have a natural resistance to fleas. Nevertheless it would be wise to treat all pets at the same time. Don't forget your cats. Cats just love to prowl the neighborhood and consequently return with unwanted guests.

Adult fleas live on the dog but their eggs drop off the dog into the environment. There they go through four larval stages before reaching adulthood, and thereby are able to jump back on the poor unsuspecting dog. The cycle resumes and takes between 21 to 28 days under ideal conditions. There are environmental products available that will kill both the adult fleas and the larvae.

Ticks

Ticks carry Rocky Mountain Spotted Fever, Lyme disease and can cause tick paralysis. They should be removed with tweezers, trying to pull out the head. The jaws carry disease. There is a tick preventive collar that does an excellent job. The ticks automatically back out on those dogs wearing collars.

Sarcoptic Mange

This is a mite that is difficult to find on skin scrapings. The pinnal reflex is a good indicator of this disease. Rub the ends of the pinna (ear) together and the dog will start scratching with his foot. Sarcoptes are highly contagious to other dogs and to humans although they do not live long on humans. They cause intense itching.

Demodectic Mange

This is a mite that is passed from the dam to her puppies. It affects youngsters age three to ten months. Diagnosis is confirmed by skin scraping. Small areas of alopecia around the eyes, lips and/or forelegs become visible. There is little itching unless there is a secondary bacterial infection. Some breeds are afflicted more than others.

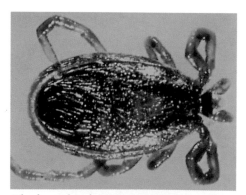

The deer tick is the most common carrier of Lyme disease. Your veterinarian can advise you if you live in an endemic area.

A bath is the perfect time to thoroughly search your Shih Tzu for parasites or skin related problems.

Cheyletiella

This causes intense itching and is diagnosed by skin scraping. It lives in the outer layers of the skin of dogs, cats, rabbits and humans. Yellow-gray scales may be found on the back and the rump, top of the head and the nose.

TO BREED OR NOT TO BREED

More than likely your breeder has requested that you have your puppy neutered or spayed. Your breeder's request is based on what is healthiest for your dog and what is most beneficial for your breed. Experienced and conscientious breeders devote many years into developing a bloodline. In order to do this, he makes every effort to plan each breeding in regard to conformation, temperament and health. This type of breeder does his best to perform the necessary testing (i.e., OFA, CERF, testing for inherited blood disorders, thyroid, etc.). Testing is expensive and sometimes very disheartening when a favorite dog doesn't pass his health tests. The health history pertains not only to the breeding stock but to the immediate ancestors. Reputable breeders do not want their offspring to be bred indiscriminately. Therefore you may be asked to neuter or spay your puppy. Of course there is always the exception, and your breeder may agree to let you breed your dog under his direct supervision. This is an important concept. More and more effort is being made to breed healthier dogs.

Since Shih Tzu are prone to a number of hereditary problems only very experienced people should breed Shih Tzu.

Spay/Neuter

There are numerous benefits of performing this surgery at six months of age. Unspayed females are subject to mammary and ovarian cancer. In order to prevent mammary cancer she must be spayed prior to her first heat cycle. Later in life, an unspayed female may develop a pyometra (an infected uterus), which is definitely life threatening.

A litter of puppies may be cute and cuddly; however, they will prove to be quite expensive by the time they go to a good home

Spaying is performed under a general anesthetic and is easy on the young dog. As you might expect it is a little harder on the older dog, but that is no reason to deny her the surgery. The surgery removes the ovaries and uterus. It is important to remove all the ovarian tissue. If some is left behind, she could remain attractive to males. In order to view the ovaries, a reasonably long incision is necessary. An ovariohysterectomy is considered major surgery.

Neutering the male at a young age will inhibit some characteristic male behavior that owners frown upon. I have found my boys will not hike their legs and mark territory if they are neutered at six months of age. Also neutering at a young age has hormonal benefits, lessening the chance of hormonal aggressiveness.

Surgery involves removing the testicles but leaving the scrotum. If there should be a retained testicle, then he definitely needs to be neutered before the age of two or three years. Retained testicles can develop into cancer. Unneutered males are at risk for testicular cancer, perineal fistulas, perianal tumors and fistulas and prostatic disease.

Intact males and females are prone to housebreaking accidents. Females urinate frequently before, during and after heat cycles, and males tend to mark territory if there is a female in heat. Males may show the same behavior if there is a visiting dog or guests.

Surgery involves a sterile operating procedure equivalent to human surgery. The incision site is shaved, surgically scrubbed and draped. The veterinarian wears a sterile surgical gown, cap, mask and gloves. Anesthesia should be monitored by a registered technician. It is customary for the veterinarian to recommend a pre-anesthetic blood screening, looking for metabolic problems and a ECG rhythm strip to check for normal heart function. Today anesthetics are equal to human anesthetics, which enables your dog to walk out of the clinic the same day as surgery.

Some folks worry about their dog's gaining weight after being neutered or spayed. This is usually not the case. It is true that some dogs may be less active so they could develop a problem, but my own dogs are just as active as they were before surgery. I have a hard time keeping weight on them. However, if your dog should begin to gain, then you need to decrease his food and see to it that he gets a little more exercise.

Medical Problems

Anal Sacs

These are small sacs on either side of the rectum that can cause the dog discomfort when they are full. They should empty when the dog has a bowel movement. Symptoms of inflammation or impaction are excessive licking under the tail and/or a bloody or sticky discharge from the anal area. Breeders like myself recommend emptying the sacs on a regular schedule when bathing the dog.

Many veterinarians prefer this isn't done unless there are symptoms. You can express the sacs by squeezing the two sacs (at the five and seven o'clock positions) in and up toward the anus. Take precautions not to get in the way of the foul-smelling fluid that is expressed. Some dogs object to this procedure so it would be wise to have someone hold

Anal sacs are not easily seen on Shih Tzu; however, if your dog begins scooting along the floor he may be trying to tell you something.

the head. Scooting is caused by anal-sac irritation and not worms.

Colitis

The stool may be frank blood or blood tinged and is the result of inflammation of the colon.

Tying your Shih Tzu puppy's topknot not only gives your puppy an adorable look but also keeps his hair from irritating his eyes.

Colitis, sometimes intermittent, can be the result of stress, undiagnosed whipworms, or perhaps idiopathic (no explainable reason). I have had several dogs prone to this disorder. They felt fine and were willing to eat but would have intermittent bloody stools. If this in an ongoing problem, you should probably feed a diet higher in fiber. Seek professional help if your dog feels poorly and/or the condition persists.

Conjunctivitis

Many breeds are prone to this problem. The conjunctiva is the pink tissue that lines the inner surface of the eyeball except the clear, transparent cornea. Irritating substances such as bacteria, foreign matter or chemicals can cause it to become reddened and swollen. It is important to keep any hair trimmed from around the eyes. Long hair stays damp and aggravates the problem. Keep the eyes cleaned with warm water and wipe away any matter that has accumulated in the corner of the eyes. If the condition persists, you should see your veterinarian. This problem goes hand in hand with keratoconjunctivitis sicca.

Ear Infection

Otitis externa is an inflammation of the external ear canal that begins at the outside opening of the ear and extends inward to the eardrum. Dogs with pendulous ears are prone to this disease, but isn't it interesting that breeds with upright ears also have a high incidence of problems? Allergies, food and inhalent, along with hormonal problems, such as hypothyroidism, are major contributors

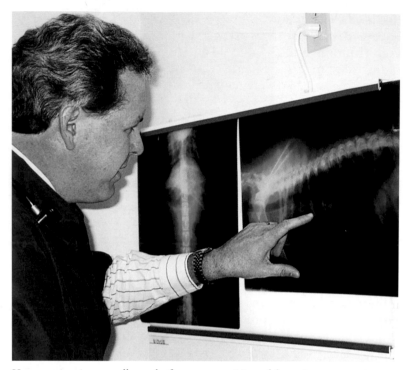

Your veterinarian can tell you a lot from an x-ray. Never delay seeing your veterinarian should you think something is wrong.

to the disease. For those dogs which have recurring problems you need to investigate the underlying cause if you hope to cure them.

I recommend that you are careful never to get water into the ears. Water provides a great medium for bacteria to grow. If your dog swims or you inadvertently get water into his ears, then use a drying agent. An at-home preparation would be to use equal parts of three-percent hydrogen peroxide and 70-percent rubbing alcohol. Another preparation is equal parts of white vinegar and water. Your veterinarian alternatively can provide a suitable product. When cleaning the ears, be careful of using cotton tip applicators since they make it easy to pack debris down into the canal. Only clean what you can see.

If your dog has an ongoing infection, don't be surprised if your veterinarian recommends sedating him and flushing his ears with a bulb syringe. Sometimes this needs to be done a few times to get the ear clean. The ear must be clean so that medication can come in contact with the canal. Be prepared to return for rechecks until the infection is gone. This may involve more flushings if the ears are very bad.

For chronic or recurring cases, your veterinarian may recommend thyroid testing, etc., and a hypoallergenic diet for a trial period of 10 to 12 weeks. Depending on your dog, it may be a good idea to see a dermatologist. Ears shouldn't be taken lightly. If the condition gets out of hand, then surgery may be necessary. Please ask your veterinarian to explain proper ear maintenance for your dog.

Flea Bite Allergy

This is the result of a hypersensitivity to the bite of a flea and its saliva. It only takes one bite to cause the dog to chew or scratch himself raw. Your dog may need medical attention to ease his discomfort. You need to clip the hair around the "hot spot" and wash it with a mild soap and water and you may need to do this daily if the area weeps. Apply an antibiotic anti-inflammatory product. Hot spots can occur from other trauma, such as grooming.

Interdigital Cysts

Check for these on your dog's feet if he shows signs of lameness. They are frequently associated with staph infections and can be quite painful. A home remedy is to soak the infected foot in a solution of a half teaspoon of bleach in a couple of quarts of water. Do this two to three times a day for a couple of days. Check with

Some Shih Tzu can be allergic to flea bites. Take caution against fleas by treating your yard regularly.

your veterinarian for an alternative remedy; antibiotics usually work well. If there is a recurring problem, surgery may be required.

Lameness

It may only be an interdigital cyst or it could be a mat between the toes, especially if your dog licks his feet.

It is wise to check over your Shih Tzu puppy daily. Check the dog's eyes, ears, feet and anus for collected matter or irritation.

Sometimes it is hard to determine which leg is affected. If he is holding up his leg, then you need to see your veterinarian.

Skin

Frequently poor skin is the result of an allergy to fleas, an inhalant allergy or food allergy. These types of problems usually result in a staph dermatitis. Dogs with food allergy usually show signs of severe itching and scratching. However, I have had some dogs with food allergies that never once itched. Their only symptom was swelling of the ears with no ear infection. Food allergy may result in recurrent bacterial skin and ear infections. Your veterinarian or dermatologist will recommend a good restricted diet. It is not wise for you to hit and miss with different dog foods. Many of the diets offered over the counter are not the hypoallergenic diet you are led to believe. Dogs acquire allergies through exposure.

Inhalant allergies result in atopy, which causes licking of the feet, scratching the body and rubbing the muzzle. It may be seasonable. Your veterinarian or dermatologist can perform intradermal testing for inhalant allergies. If your dog should test positive, then a vaccine may be prepared. The results are very satisfying.

RESOURCES

American Shih Tzu Club, Inc.
Corresponding Secreatry: Bonnie Prato
5252 Shafer Avenue
Oakland, CA 94618-1051
www.clubs.akc.org/astc/index.html

American Kennel Club
260 Madison Avenue
New York, NY 10016
or 5580 Centerview Drive
Raleigh, NC 27606
(919) 233-9767
(919) 816-3627
www.akc.org

The United Kennel Club, Inc.
100 E. Kilgore Road
Kalamazoo, Michigan 49002-5584
(616) 343-9020
www.ukcdogs.com

The Kennel Club
1 Clarges Street
Picadilly, London WIY 8AB, England
www.the-kennel-club.org.uk

The Canadian Kennel Club
89 Skyway Avenue
Suite 100
Etobicoke, Ontarion, Canada M9W 6R4
www.ckc.ca

INDEX